Revise for Geography GCSE SEG Syllabus A

Ann Bowen

John Pallister

Heinemann Educational Publishers
Halley Court
Jordan Hill
Oxford
OX2 8EJ

Heinemann is a registered trade mark of
Reed Educational & Professional Publishing Ltd

OXFORD   MELBOURNE   AUCKLAND
JOHANNESBURG   BLANTYRE   GABORONE
IBADAN   PORTSMOUTH NH (USA)   CHICAGO

Text © Ann Bowen and John Pallister

First published 1999

02
10 9 8 7 6 5 4

British Library Cataloguing in Publication Data
A catalogue record for this book is available from the British Library

ISBN 0 435 10117 X

Typeset and designed by Magnet Harlequin, Oxford

Printed and bound in the UK by Bath Colour Books

Acknowledgements
The publishers would like to thank the following for permission to reproduce copyright material.

Maps and diagrams:
Edward Arnold Ltd (Fig 3, p46); Financial Times (Fig 2, p100); Hodder & Stoughton (Fig 1, p7);
Longman (Fig 2, p8), (Fig 2, p26), (Fig 3, p117); Nelson (Fig 3, p61), (Fig 1, p70); Northumbrian Water
Authority (Fig 3, p27); Oliver & Boyd (Fig 1, p8), (Fig 1, p59), Fig 1, p82); Ordnance Survey (Fig 3,
p115); Penguin Books Ltd (Fig 4, p117); Routledge (Fig 1, p106); Schofield & Sims Ltd (Fig 2, p113);
Shell International (Fig 2, p108); Stanley Thornes (Fig 1, p84); The Guardian (Fig 2, p49), (Fig 2, p105);
Time International Magazine (Fig 3, p95); UN Population Division (Fig 2, p71), (Fig 1, p95);
Unwin Hyman Ltd (Fig 1, p46), (Fig 2, p61)

Photographs:
Aerofilms (Fig 1, p114), (Fig 1, p116); EOSAT (Fig 4, p119); University of Dundee (Fig 5, p119)

The publishers have made every effort to trace the copyright holders, but if they have inadvertently
overlooked any, they will be pleased to make the necessary arrangements at the first opportunity.

Contents

How to use this book

Revise for Geography GCSE has been written to help you revise successfully for your GCSE Geography examination. It has been designed to meet the requirements of the SEG A Syllabus although it is also suitable for other GCSE syllabuses. The revision book supports the text book *Understanding GCSE Geography*.

SEG Syllabus A

The syllabus includes:
1 Natural environment topics
2 Human geography topics
3 Skills including Ordnance Survey maps
4 Coursework.

1 *Natural environment topics*
You need to study a minimum of **three** of the following natural environment topics:

Tectonic activity	☐	Coasts ☐
Rocks and landscapes	☐	Weather and climate ☐
River processes and features	☐	Ecosystems ☐
Ice	☐	

Tick the boxes to indicate which topics you have studied in class. These are the ones you need to revise and the only topics you should answer questions on in the examination.

2 *Human geography topics*
You need to study a minimum of **three** of the following human geography topics, one from each pair:

One from	Population	☐
or	Settlement	☐
One from	Agriculture	☐
or	Industry	☐
One from	Managing resources and tourism	☐
or	Development and interdependence	☐

3 *Skills for SEG Syllabus A*
Section A of the first written examination paper has three structured questions testing geographical skills. These skills are covered in Chapter 14, especially those connected with maps and photographs. The chapter includes a check-list of all the skills you may need in the examination. The list does not include the techniques and skills connected solely with data collection for fieldwork.

4 *The coursework*
Paper 1 is the coursework which may be one or two geographical enquiries. It is worth 25% of the final mark. This revision guide does not cover the coursework, which should be more or less complete by the time you are starting to revise for your final examinations.

Case studies
Within the physical and human geography topics there are a series of Key Ideas to be studied. You need to understand the Key Ideas and be able to apply them to case studies of real places that you have studied.

Case studies are a very important part of any geography syllabus. They are studies of real places. For example, having looked at general ideas about how a coastline is eroded and the features which are formed, you could then study a stretch of coastline such as the Yorkshire coast to see how all of the ideas come together to produce a landscape.

SEG Syllabus A does not set any particular case studies or examples to illustrate the topics. It leaves the choice of case study open. Usually the teacher chooses a good example which s/he knows well or for which there are good up-to-date resources available. The selection of case studies in this book is based upon those used in *Understanding GCSE Geography*. The case studies are topical and good examples of the theme being studied. However, you may have studied some different case studies during your course. Don't worry about it. You can either choose to learn the ones you have already studied and been taught or you can use the new ones in the book.   However, learning new case studies at this stage of the course could mean extra work and may even be confusing.

How is SEG Syllabus A assessed?

There are three parts to the assessment for SEG A: coursework and two written papers. The written papers are tiered.

Tiering

Hopefully, while studying your GCSE Geography, you have completed exercises, tests and practice questions. The results from these should indicate to you what sort of grade you are capable of achieving in the examination. This is important because you will be entered for either the Foundation or the Higher Tier Papers.

The Foundation Tier covers grades from C to G. Questions on the papers are often shorter and more help is given to the students. There is less extended writing. The Higher Tier covers grades A* to D. An E grade has been allowed in recent years but this may not continue. Questions on the Higher Tier require more extended writing and there are fewer short-answer questions. Some parts of the questions may be on both the Higher and Foundation Tier papers.

Written component 1:
Papers 2 (Foundation Tier) and 3 (Higher Tier)
Written component one has two sections, A and B, both containing a series of structured questions. The paper lasts for 1 hour 45 minutes. There is a total of 73 marks on the paper which includes 4 marks for spelling, grammar, punctuation and the use of specialist terms (SPaG). The paper is worth 40% of the final mark.

Section A tests skills and will always include an Ordnance Survey map at either the 1:50 000 or 1: 25 000 scale. There may also be questions based on photographs, other maps, graphs and data. The questions are worth a total of 24 marks.

Section B includes seven structured questions each worth 15 marks. There is one question on each of the natural environment topics. You choose to answer three only. Every year some candidates make the mistake of trying to answer all seven; the results are always disappointing because usually they have not been taught all seven and none of the answers are detailed enough to gain good marks.

Questions in the examination will often say ... 'Using examples from your studies'... You must be able to give detailed knowledge about real places in your examination answers.

Hints and Tips!

Where possible, it is usually an advantage to use case studies which are local to you. But always stick to the case studies you have been taught and have studied in class. If the ones in this book match, then it's a bonus!

Written component 2:
Papers 4 (Foundation Tier) and 5 (Higher Tier)

This paper has three sections and you answer one question from each section. Each question is worth 25 marks and the paper lasts for 1 hour 30 minutes.

Questions include resources such as maps, photographs and diagrams and the questions are structured. There are fewer skills marks on this paper so there are more questions requiring knowledge and understanding.

How to use the book

Revise for Geography GCSE has been written to cover all elements of the written papers of the SEG A Examination Syllabus.

- Chapter 14 covers the skills especially important for Section A on the written papers of the first written paper.
- Chapters 1 to 7 cover the seven natural environment topics also examined on the first written paper.
- Chapters 8 to 13 cover the six human topics examined on the second written paper. Each chapter includes resources and activities to encourage you to develop your technique in answering GCSE-style questions.

Throughout the book there are hints and tips to improve your revision and examination technique. Special notes are included on the right hand side of most of the pages in the book. You have already come across some of these:

Extra information and useful facts and ideas to help you with your examination answers.

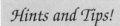

These give general advice and useful information to help you prepare for and sit the examination. Following the advice could stop you wasting time and improve your grade.

Things to do: boxes to tick to check your progress, gaps to fill in, activities to focus your revision to improve that grade. If you do well, be pleased with yourself. If at first you don't do well, re-read the section and test yourself again.

All the chapters include some practice questions similar to those you will face in the examination. Each question includes the number of marks you can hope to achieve. Pages 123-7 give mark schemes for the test questions and lots of other useful advice on the best way to answer questions – and even how not to answer them!

Finally...

Good luck. Work hard, but...

- Try to enjoy your revision. It should be satisfying to see the whole subject come together at the end of the course. You become a real geographer and real geographers impress examiners.
- Plan your revision carefully. Be methodical and work steadily. Desperate last minute cramming leads to panic!

Hints and Tips!

Half an hour per question – almost a mark a minute! Work carefully but keep an eye on the clock. Always aim to finish three whole questions.

Hints and Tips!

In the examination, if you run out of space for your answer ask for an extra sheet to write on – and remember to clearly label the question number and part. If you only have a few more words to write there is usually enough space to fit them alongside or under the answer in the booklet without using an extra sheet.

Hints and Tips!

Take special note of how many marks each part of a question has and how many lines have been allocated. This tells you how much information and detail you need to include in your answer. A two word answer will not gain many marks in an 8 mark question!

1 Tectonic activity

A 15 mark question on this topic will be Question 4 of section B on your first examination paper.

Key Ideas
1 The Earth's crust is unstable.
2 Tectonic activity influences human activity.

Key words and definitions

acid lava	thick, viscous lava with a high silica content, flows short distances
basic lava	thin 'runny' lava, low silica content, flows long distances
composite volcano	steep-sided cone with layers of ash and lava
compressional margin	where two plates are moving together (destructive)
earthquake	a shaking of the Earth's crust
fold mountains	mountains formed by plate movements
Richter Scale	measures the strength of an earthquake
shield volcano	gentle sides, wide base made of basic lava
tectonic plate	a huge section of the Earth's crust
tensional margin	where two plates are moving apart (constructive)
volcano	a cone-shaped mountain created by lava from repeated eruptions

Key Ideas:

What you need to study and to know:
- there are several large tectonic plates which may move together, move apart or slide past each other;
- the movement of the plates causes the formation of fold mountains, volcanoes and earthquakes;
- there are three main types of volcano – composite, acid lava and shield volcanoes – each with different characteristics;
- earthquakes are measured using the Richter Scale;
- human activities in fold mountains, such as the Alps, include tourism, HEP, farming and forestry;
- there are both advantages and disadvantages for settlement in areas of tectonic activity;
- the effects of, and responses to, earthquakes and volcanoes may be different in MEDCs and LEDCs.

Cover up the definitions of the key words and see how many you know.

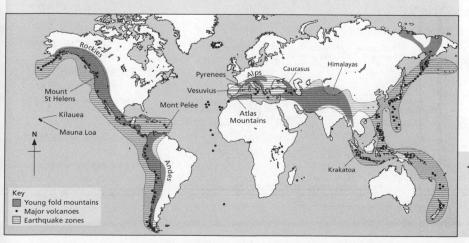

Key
- Young fold mountains
- Major volcanoes
- Earthquake zones

◀ Figure 1 shows the world distribution of fold mountains, active volcanoes and earthquake zones.

Tectonic plates

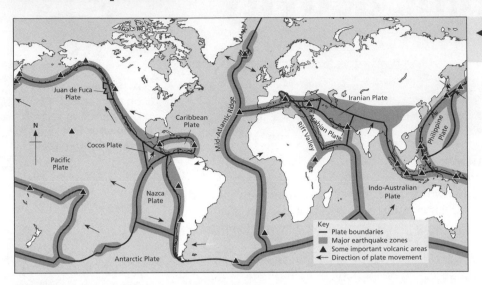

Convection currents are very hot currents moving upwards in the mantle.

The mantle is a deep layer of molten rock below the Earth's crust

The Earth's crust is not one continuous layer; it is made up of several tectonic plates. The plates move in response to convection currents in the mantle so the Earth's crust is unstable. Movement has the greatest impact at plate boundaries, where two plates meet.

Compressional plate boundaries
- Plates move together
- One plate sinks below the other
- The plate melts in the subduction zone where there is great heat and pressure
- Energy may be released as an earthquake
- The molten rock or magma may rise forming composite volcanoes
- The lighter crust at the surface may crumple to form fold mountains

A compressional plate boundary

Tensional plate boundaries
- Plates move apart
- Gap filled by rising magma from the mantle
- Rising magma forms shield volcanoes
- Most common under oceans so submarine volcanoes or volcanic islands are formed
- Plates buckle to form ridges

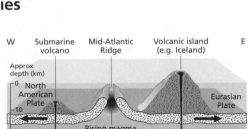
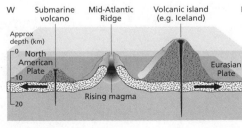

A tensional plate boundary

▲ *Figure 2 What happens at plate boundaries?*

Test Yourself

1 Add the following labels to Figure 1 to complete the naming of the tectonic plates.

   North American Plate
   South American Plate
   African Plate
   Eurasian Plate

2 Use Figure 1 to name two plates which form:
(a) a compressional plate boundary
(b) a tensional plate boundary.

3 Name an example of :
(a) a composite volcano
(b) a shield volcano
(c) an oceanic ridge
(d) a volcanic island.

The Alps – a range of fold mountains

Why are they there?
The Alps lie along a compressional plate boundary where, for ten million years, two plates pushed together. The rocks were folded upwards forming simple folds, overfolds and nappes.

What are the physical features of the Alps?
- high mountains, e.g. Mont Blanc (4810m)
- steep slopes
- deep valleys, e.g. Lauterbrunnen
- lakes, e.g. Lake Como
- source area for rivers, e.g. the Rhine

Fold mountains

Fold mountains form along plate boundaries as a result of great Earth movements (Figure 3).

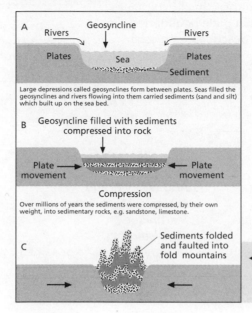

A — Large depressions called geosynclines form between plates. Seas filled the geosynclines and rivers flowing into them carried sediments (sand and silt) which built up on the sea bed.

B — Geosyncline filled with sediments compressed into rock

Over millions of years the sediments were compressed, by their own weight, into sedimentary rocks, e.g. sandstone, limestone.

C — Sediments folded and faulted into fold mountains

Figure 3 The formation of fold mountains

1 Write down at least two examples of fold mountains and their locations.

2 Practice drawing and labelling the diagrams to show the formation of fold mountains. Make sure you can also describe and explain how they are formed.

What are the human activities in the Alps?

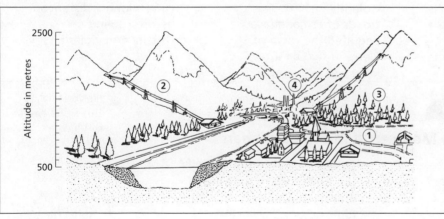

Figure 4 An Alpine valley

Match the numbers on Figure 4 with the correct human activity in the box below.

A Farming
- Mostly on the valley floor where it is flatter, more sheltered, warmer, with deeper soils
- Traditionally dairying
- Main crops are hay and cereals with some vines and fruit in warmer areas
- Use upland pastures in summer

B Tourism
Tourists are attracted by:
- Winter resorts, e.g. Chamonix, St Moritz
- Summer resorts, e.g. Lake Garda
- Winter sports, e.g. skiing, tobogganing
- Beautiful scenery and the Alpine climate
- Ease of access through good communications, e.g. Simplon pass, Geneva airport

C HEP and industry
- Industry needing large amounts of electricity, e.g. sawmills, smelters locate near to HEP stations which generate cheap electricity from the fast flowing streams
- Traditional industries include clock making, paper and furniture

D Forestry
- Conifers cover the slopes up to about 1800 metres. The wood is used for fuel, building chalets and for paper making.

Volcanoes

Types of volcano

Composite cone volcanoes usually form at compressional plate boundaries. Shield volcanoes usually form along tensional plate boundaries. The formation of both types is described on page 8.

Test Yourself

1 Draw and label a cross-section through a volcano to show its main characteristics.
2 Cover up the case study on Montserrat. Write down four effects of the eruption and four responses to the eruption.

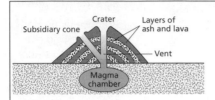
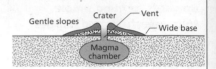

Composite cone volcano
Examples: Mount Etna, Vesuvius, Mount St Helens
Characteristics:
- Steep-sided symmetrical cone shape
- High with narrow base
- Alternate layers of acid lava and ash
- Lava may cool inside the vent – the next eruption is very explosive to remove the plug
- Subsidiary cones and vents form.

Acid lava volcano
Example: Mont Pelée, in Martinique
Characteristics:
- Very steep cone or spine with narrow base
- Composed of acid lava which does not flow easily
- Very explosive eruptions: Mont Pelée erupted very violently in 1902. The clouds of ash and lava engulfed the town of St Pierre in two minutes, killing 30 000 people.

Shield volcano (basic lava)
Examples: Mauna Loa and Kilauea, both on the Hawaiian Islands
Characteristics:
- Gentle slopes and wide base
- Frequent eruptions of basic lava
- Lava flows more easily, travels longer distances before cooling
- Usually non-violent.

▲ *Figure 1 Different types of volcano*

Know your case study

Volcanic eruptions on Montserrat in the Caribbean

Effects of the eruptions
- Plymouth, the capital city, covered in ash – became a ghost town
- Villages destroyed – people made homeless
- 23 people killed
- Forest fires
- Floods as valleys were blocked by ash
- Airport and port closed
- Farmland destroyed
- Tourist industry stopped
- Industries crippled

Responses to the eruptions by the local people
- Evacuation of over 5000 people abroad, some to Britain
- Others moved to the north of the Island where they lived in makeshift camps
- Riots occurred as locals complained that the British government was not doing enough.

Responses to the eruption by the governments in Montserrat and Britain
- £41 million of aid given
- Temporary shelters provided
- Money given to the people to help them move to other countries
- Free flights out of the island.

Hints and Tips!

If you are asked to use examples or case studies make sure you include specific facts and details. When the examiners read your answer they will ask themselves is this really about Montserrat or could it be about any volcanic eruption. Learn and include the place names and figures to make it real.

Earthquakes

Earthquakes are vibrations in the Earth's crust. The vibrations usually occur along a fault or plate boundary (Figure 3). The plates become jammed together. The pressure builds up until eventually the friction is overcome and the plates jerk past each other. These sudden movements cause the earthquake.

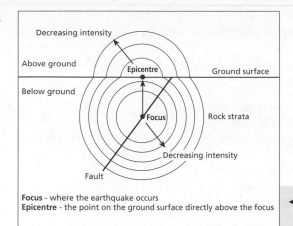

Focus - where the earthquake occurs
Epicentre - the point on the ground surface directly above the focus

◀ *Figure 2 The features of an earthquake*

Measuring earthquakes

The magnitude of an earthquake is recorded using an instrument called a seismograph, and given a value between 1-10 on the Richter Scale. The scale is logarithmic: an earthquake measuring 6 is 10 times more powerful than one measuring 5.

90 per cent of all earthquakes occur along compressional plate boundaries. These are also the most violent earthquakes.

Know your case study

An Earthquake – Kobe, Japan 1995

Causes
Kobe lies close to a short fault line between the Philippine and south Japan tectonic plates. The two plates are sliding past each other. This is called a passive plate boundary. In January 1995 about 50km of the fault moved causing the Great Hanshin earthquake.

Effects

Primary (the immediate damage)
Over 100 000 houses collapsed
Loss of life – 5500 people killed
30 000 people injured
Roads and railways wrecked
Electricity, gas and sewerage systems destroyed
10% schools destroyed
12% industry and 14% services destroyed
Emergency services disrupted

Secondary (the after effects)
300 000 people homeless
Landslides
Huge fires
Stress and shock
Two million homes without power
One million homes with no water for ten days
Health hazards in the makeshift shelters
A flu epidemic

Responses

Emergency Action
Emergency services and the army brought in from other areas to help
Heat seeking equipment to find people
Emergency shelters
Mobile telephone systems
Water and food supplies brought in
Hospitals set up in schools
Putting out fires

Medium/long-term plans
Bulldozing unsafe buildings
Rebuilding homes, schools, roads, hospitals etc.
Repairing water, electricity, phone and sewerage systems
Provide help for those in shock
More monitoring equipment
Introduce an emergency action plan

Cover up this page and then try to answer these questions.

(a) Explain how an earthquake happens.
(b) Name the scale used to measure earthquakes.
(c) Give four primary and four secondary effects of the Kobe earthquake.
(d) Give four responses to the earthquake in Kobe.

The impact of tectonic activity

Why do so many people choose to live in earthquake zones or near volcanoes?

Despite the threat of earthquakes and eruptions many people do live in areas of tectonic activity, but why?

Near volcanoes there may be many advantages:
- fertile soils when the lava weathers;
- jobs in tourism, e.g. trips to see the crater, souvenir shops and hotel accommodation;
- minerals, e.g. sulphur and pumice;
- hot springs for bathing and heating;
- heat used to generate electricity.

The impact of earthquakes and volcanoes is often much more severe:
- in urban areas rather than rural areas;
- in LEDCs rather than MEDCs.

The magnitude of the earthquake is often less important than where the earthquake occurs. You need to know why! Think about the density of population, the types of buildings, the availability of emergency services and early warning systems and communications.

Know your case study

Vesuvius and the Plain of Campania for the advantages of living near volcanoes

Fertile soils – for wheat, tomatoes, peaches, almonds and vines with yields five times higher than the national average;

Tourism – trips to Vesuvius and hot springs, museums at Pompeii and Herculaneum;

Minerals – the sulphur wasteland nearby at the Phlegraean Fields.

Remember, for some people it may be the best farmland available; that was certainly the case on Montserrat and near Vesuvius. Some people may not be able to afford to move anywhere else. Others may believe that an eruption or earthquake will never happen in their lifetime.

Examination practice question

1 Study Figure 1 showing information about four earthquakes.

Figure 1

Year	Location	Strength (Richter Scale)	Approx. number of deaths	Rural or urban	MEDC or LEDC
1964	Anchorage, Alaska	8.4	1	Rural	MEDC
1995	Kobe, Japan	7.2	5500	Urban	MEDC
1960	Chile	9.5	5700	Rural	LEDC
1970	Ancash, Peru	7.8	66 000	Urban	LEDC

(a) (i) Name the country with the earthquake of greatest strength as measured on the Richter Scale. *(1 mark)*

   (ii) What does Figure 1 show about the relationship between the strength of an earthquake and the number of deaths. *(2 marks)*

(b) Explain why the death toll from an earthquake is usually higher in urban areas and in LEDCs. *(6 marks)*

(c) (i) Name and locate a range of fold mountains you have studied. *(2 marks)*

   (ii) With the aid of diagrams, describe how fold mountains are formed. *(4 marks)*

[Check your answers on page 123]   Total = 15 marks

Summary

Key words from the syllabus

acid lava	continental plate	shield volcano
basic lava	earthquake	tectonic activity
composite volcano	fold mountains	tensional margin
compressional margin	Richter Scale	volcano

Checklist for revision

	Understand and know	Need more revision	Do not understand	Hints and tips
I know the names of several large plates making up the Earth's surface	☐	☐	☐	p 6
I can recognise a compressional and tensional plate margin	☐	☐	☐	pp 6-7
I know what happens at different plate margins and the features produced	☐	☐	☐	pp 6-7, 12
I know the world distribution and formation of fold mountains	☐	☐	☐	p 8
I know the world distribution of volcanoes	☐	☐	☐	p 8
I know the reasons why they are located at plate boundaries	☐	☐	☐	p 12
I know the appearance/formation of:				
• acid lava volcanoes	☐	☐	☐	p 13
• shield volcanoes	☐	☐	☐	
• composite volcanoes	☐	☐	☐	
I know the world distribution of earthquakes	☐	☐	☐	p 8
I know why they are located near plate boundaries	☐	☐	☐	p 16
I know reasons why tectonic events have different effects in:				
• LEDCs and MEDCs	☐	☐	☐	p 17
• urban and rural areas	☐	☐	☐	

Test Yourself

Write down a definition for each of the key words. Check them with those given on page 7.

Hints and Tips!

The page numbers refer to where the topic can be found in your text book *Understanding GCSE Geography*. If you don't understand the topic read the relevant section in your text book, make some notes and learn about it.

Test Yourself

Tick the boxes and fill in the gaps – if you still do not understand seek help from your teacher.

Know your case studies

Which real places have you studied as an example of...

- human activity in an area of fold mountains　　name:_____　pp 10-11
- an earthquake – causes, effects and responses　name:_____　pp 16-17
- a volcanic eruption – causes, effects, responses　name:_____　pp 12-15
- the advantages and disadvantages of living near a volcano　　name:_____　p 18

2 Rocks and landscape

Key Ideas
1 The Earth's crust is made of different rock types which form distinctive landscapes.
2 The Earth's crust is changed by weathering processes.
Each key idea will be looked at in turn.

A question on this topic appears in Section B in your first written paper.

It is a 15 mark question and it will be Question 5.

Key words and definitions

Carboniferous limestone	sedimentary rock made of beds of lime
chemical weathering	breakdown of rock as a result of changes in the composition of the rock
economic use of a rock	what the rock can be used for
exfoliation	peeling off of the outer layers of a rock by alternate heating and cooling
freeze-thaw	breakdown of rock by changes in temperature above and below freezing point
igneous rock	rock formed by the cooling of hot magma
land uses	ways of using the land such as settlement, farming and quarrying
limestone solution	process by which acidic rain water dissolves limestone rock
metamorphic rock	rocks changed by heat and pressure into a different form
physical weathering	breakdown of rock without any change in its composition
quarrying	removing rock from the ground surface
sedimentary rock	rock formed from materials deposited on the sea bed

Key Idea 1: the Earth's crust is made of different rock types which form distinctive landscapes
What you need to study and to know:
- the three groups of rocks are igneous, sedimentary and metamorphic;
- granite is a hard igneous rock which forms upland landscapes with landforms such as tors;
- Carboniferous limestone is a sedimentary rock which weathers to form karst scenery;
- chalk and clay are also sedimentary rocks which erode to form scarp and vale scenery;
- these rocks have economic uses.

Put a piece of paper over the definitions. Test yourself again after you have read the chapter.

Igneous, sedimentary and metamorphic rocks

Rock group	Definition	Example(s)	Name of area
Igneous	see above	Granite	Dartmoor
Sedimentary	see above	Carboniferous limestone	Yorkshire Dales (e.g. around Malham)
		Chalk	South Downs
		Clay	London Basin
Metamorphic	see above	Slate	North Wales

Granite landscapes

Certain characteristics of granite (lettered **A – C** below) have major effects on the landscape.

A Granite is a hard rock

It forms upland areas, such as Dartmoor, because it resists erosion. Around the coast, granite forms rugged cliffs such as at Land's End.

B Granite is an impermeable rock

There are many marshy areas and bogs on the flat topped uplands because little water is absorbed into the rock. There are many surface streams on Dartmoor which have cut steep sided V-shaped valleys such as the River Dart.

C Granite has many joints

Joints are important in the formation of tors. Joints are vertical lines of weakness in the rock which can be attacked by freeze-thaw weathering.

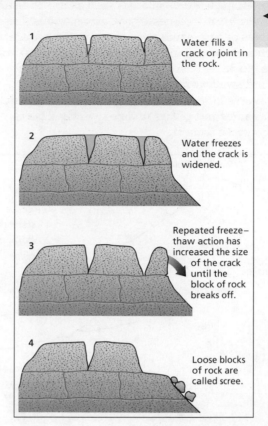

1 Water fills a crack or joint in the rock.

2 Water freezes and the crack is widened.

3 Repeated freeze–thaw action has increased the size of the crack until the block of rock breaks off.

4 Loose blocks of rock are called scree.

◀ *Figure 1 Freeze-thaw weathering*

Did you know how freeze-thaw weathering operates? Look at Figure 1.

Stage 1 – water fills a joint or crack in the rock

Stage 2 – water in the joint freezes, expands and widens the joint

Stage 3 – freezing and thawing repeated many times increases the size of the joint…

Stage 4 … until the block of rock breaks off

Formation of tors

- weathering by freeze-thaw is rapid where the joints are close together
- there are plenty of cracks for water to seep into and expand when it freezes
- repeated freezing and thawing widens the joints and pieces of rock break off
- the rock is weathered less quickly where the joints are wide apart
- blocks of rock, called tors, are left where the joints are wide apart

Cover up Figure 1.

Draw your own labelled diagrams for freeze-thaw weathering.

Hints and Tips!

You will also need to know about the freeze-thaw process if you study the topic of 'Ice' (Chapter 4).

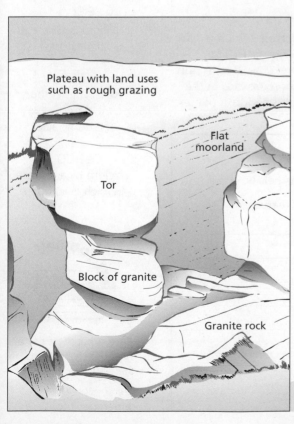

Plateau with land uses such as rough grazing

Flat moorland

Tor

Block of granite

Granite rock

◀ *Figure 2 Granite scenery*

Carboniferous limestone landscapes

You cannot mistake the landscape features in areas such as the Yorkshire Dales and Peak District where great thicknesses of Carboniferous limestone outcrop. There are large areas of bare white rock covering the surface; these are the limestone pavements broken up into separate blocks (clints) with gaps (grykes) between the blocks. Any surface rivers soon disappear underground down sink and swallow holes. If you have visited underground caves and caverns to see the amazing and wonderful shapes formed by stalactites, stalagmites and pillars of lime, you have been amongst Carboniferous limestone scenery.

Hints and Tips!

Stala**c**tites hang down from the **c**eiling of the cave.

Stala**g**mites grow up from the **g**round.

Grykes are the **g**aps between the limestone blocks.

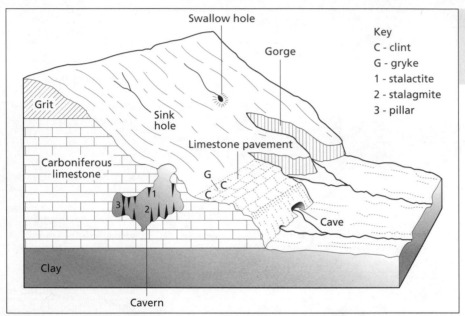

Key
C - clint
G - gryke
1 - stalactite
2 - stalagmite
3 - pillar

◀ *Figure 1 Carboniferous limestone (karst) scenery*

Carboniferous limestone is dissolved by chemical weathering, which is why such distinctive landscapes of karst scenery are formed (Figure 1). The weathering process is called limestone solution. Limestone dissolves in rain water which is slightly acidic. Rainwater mixes with carbon dioxide in the air to form carbonic acid which attacks the many joints and bedding planes in the limestone and dissolves the rock.

You can use the chemical formula for limestone solution if you prefer.

$CaCO_3$
calcium carbonate (limestone)
+
H_2CO_3
water and carbon dioxide (carbonic acid)
↓
$Ca(HCO_3)_2$
calcium bicarbonate (which is soluble)

Activity: definitions

Match the features named in Figure 1 to the definitions below.

Definition	Name of feature
Small underground passage ways	_____
Large underground chamber	_____
Steep-sided rocky valley	_____
Flat surfaces of bare blocks of rock	_____
Column of lime hanging from the roof	_____
Column of lime built up from the floor	_____
Funnel-shaped hole down which a stream disappears underground	_____

Test Yourself

Place a piece of paper over the definitions of the features.

See if you can remember them.

In many places in southern and eastern England chalk and clay rocks outcrop next to each other. They are both sedimentary rocks, but have little else in common.

Chalk	Clay
Chalk resists erosion and forms upland areas, e.g. the South Downs	Clay is a soft rock which has been eroded to form lowland areas, e.g. the London Basin
Chalk is porous and there are few surface rivers to help to erode it, e.g. Devil's Dyke is a dry valley	Clay is impervious and there are many surface rivers, e.g. the River Thames and its tributaries
Chalk forms an escarpment with its steep scarp slope and gentle dip slope, e.g. the scarp of the South Downs faces north	Clay forms vales which are wide areas of flat lowland, e.g. as you leave the London Basin the land rises up to the Chilterns and North Downs
At the coast there are landforms of erosion such as cliffs and stacks, e.g. Beachy Head	Coastlines are low and flat with large muddy river estuaries, e.g. the Thames estuary

Hints and Tips!

Make sure you can also name examples of areas of granite and Carboniferous limestone and of their main features, as has been done for chalk and clay in this table.

Formation of chalk escarpments
- there needs to be beds of rock dip at an angle to the ground surface.
- there needs to be alternate bands of chalk and clay.
- clay is a soft rock and is eroded more quickly than the chalk.
- clay vales, which are flat lowland areas, form.
- chalk resists erosion longer than the clay.
- chalk escarpments are left as upland areas between the clay vales.
- the gentle slope follows the dip of the rocks.

Test Yourself

1 Figure 2 is a sketch map of an area of chalk and clay. Some of the features have been lettered A – D. Match the letter to the landform.

Landform	Letter
Flat lowland	_____
Scarp slope	_____
Dry valley	_____
Dip slope	_____

2 On Figure 2:
(a) label the chalk escarpment;
(b) shade in the area without surface rivers.

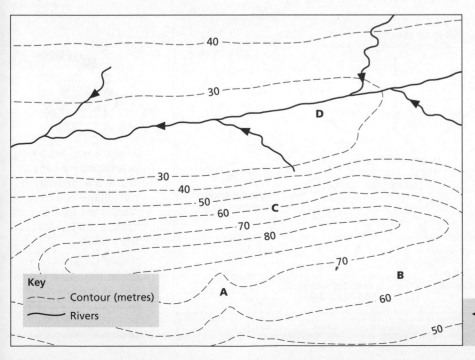

Key
— — — Contour (metres)
——— Rivers

◀ Figure 2 Contour sketch map

Economic uses of rocks

Rocks from which to make stones for building have been quarried for centuries. Houses, churches and walls are usually built out of local stone. Today most quarries are operated by large companies which make good profits from selling rocks and stones.

Rock	Economic uses
Granite	Building stone, bedding for railway tracks, sea defences It weathers into china clay used for pottery and various products
Limestone	Building stone, dry stone walls, making cement It is also used as a cleanser in steel works and power stations
Chalk	Building stone (especially where flints are found in the chalk) Making cement
Clay	Making bricks, with many brick works in the clay vale between Oxford and Peterborough

Aberdeen is known as the 'granite city'.

The Houses of Parliament are built of limestone.

Unfortunately, quarrying rocks brings several problems.
- As the site is being prepared, farming is disrupted, natural habitats are lost and the area's scenic beauty is marred.
- When the quarry is working there are problems from noise, dust and dirt, and heavy lorries on the roads. The quarry is also unsightly.
- When the quarrying stops, a great scar is left on the landscape. Landfill may take many years and it may have harmful effects.

Although a few local people may gain employment, most of the work is done by machines rather than people. However, there are ways in which the effects of some of the problems can be reduced (Figure 1).

Write down as many causes as you can of the following problems which are linked to quarrying:
- noise
- dust and dirt
- looks unsightly

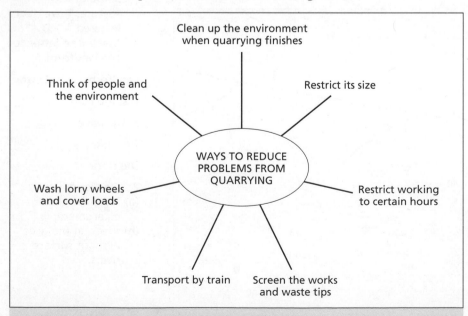

▲ Figure 1 Ways to reduce the problems of quarrying

Imagine you are living in a country village. There is a meeting in the village hall to discuss the proposal to open a quarry next to the village.

In two columns, write down the views that the village people are likely to express FOR and AGAINST the proposal.

Key Idea 2: the Earth's crust is changed by weathering processes
What you need to study and to know:

Definition of weathering
Weathering is the breakdown of surface rocks for which the weather is mainly responsible. It is different from erosion because the rocks are broken down where they lie without being transported.

Physical weathering
You need to know two types.
1 Freeze-thaw which was explained on page 15; the sharp-edged pieces of rock broken off by it form scree.
2 Exfoliation which mainly takes place in deserts; after many years of great heating by day and cooling at night the outer layer of the rock peels away to leave a smaller rounded boulder.

Chemical weathering
We have referred to two types.
1 Chemical weathering leading to breakdown of the minerals in granite to give china clay.
2 Limestone solution which leads to distinctive landforms both on the surface and underground in areas of Carboniferous limestone.

DID YOU KNOW?

With **physical weathering** the rock breaks up without any change to the rock itself. Pieces of rock are simply broken off.

With **chemical weathering**, the nature of the rock is changed. Limestone is changed from calcium carbonate into calcium bicarbonate by rain water which is acidic.

Hints and Tips!

Memory aid: exfoliation weathering is like peeling off the layers of an onion.

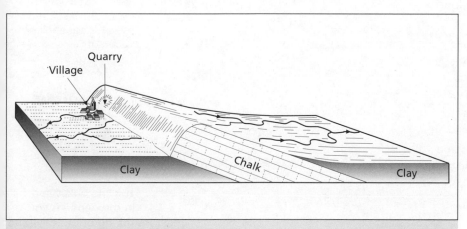

▲ *Figure 2 A chalk escarpment*

Examination practice question

Figure 2 shows the lay out of rocks in parts of southern England.

(a) Chalk and clay are both sedimentary rocks.
   Where and how do sedimentary rocks form?   (2 marks)

(b) (i) On Figure 2 label the following landforms:
       scarp slope; dip slope; vale.   (3 marks)

   (ii) Explain how the chalk escarpment was formed.   (4 marks)

(c) (i) State two reasons why chalk is quarried.   (2 marks)

   (ii) Explain some of the disadvantages for people living in the village next to the quarry on Figure 2.   (4 marks)

[Check your answers on page 123]   Total =15 marks

Summary

Key words from the syllabus

Carboniferous limestone	freeze-thaw	metamorphic rock
chemical weathering	igneous rocks	physical weathering
economic use of a rock	land uses	quarrying
exfoliation	limestone solution	sedimentary rock

Checklist for revision

	Understand and know	Need more revision	Do not understand	Hints and tips
I can name three types of rock	☐	☐	☐	p 20
I can name rock examples of each type	☐	☐	☐	p 20
I can describe the features of granite landscapes	☐	☐	☐	p 22
I can explain the formation of tors	☐	☐	☐	p 22
I can describe features of Carboniferous limestone scenery	☐	☐	☐	p 24
I understand limestone solution	☐	☐	☐	p 24
I know the economic uses of limestone	☐	☐	☐	p 25
I can describe the features of a chalk escarpment	☐	☐	☐	p 26
I can explain the differences in settlement and land uses between areas of chalk and clay	☐	☐	☐	p 27
I understand the advantages and disadvantages of quarrying	☐	☐	☐	p 28
I can give a definition of weathering	☐	☐	☐	p 30
I understand the difference between physical and chemical weathering	☐	☐	☐	p 30
I can explain how freeze-thaw works	☐	☐	☐	p 22

Test Yourself

Write down a definition for each of the key words. Check them with those given on page 14.

Hints and Tips!

The page numbers refer to where the topic can be found in your text book *Understanding GCSE Geography*. If you don't understand the topic read the relevant section in your text book, make some notes and learn about it.

Test Yourself

Tick the boxes and fill in the gaps – if you still do not understand seek help from your teacher.

Know your case studies

Which real places have you studied as an example of...

• a granite landscape	name:_____	p 23
• Carboniferous limestone scenery	name:_____	p 25
• chalk and clay scenery	name:_____	pp 26-7
• quarrying	name:_____	p 29

3 River processes and features

Key Ideas
1 River processes produce distinctive landforms.
2 Landscape features affect human activities.
Each key idea will be looked at in turn.

A 15 mark question on this topic will be Question 6 of Section B in your first written paper.

Key Idea 1: river processes produce distinctive landforms
What you need to study and to know:

A River erosion and resulting landforms
- the four main processes of river erosion are hydraulic power, corrosion, corrasion and attrition;
- most river erosion takes place in the upper course of a river;
- the distinctive landforms formed by river erosion are waterfalls and gorges and the V-shaped valley cross-section found in the upper course.

B Processes of river transport
- materials are transported by four main processes – boulders rolling, saltation, suspension and solution.

C River deposition and resulting landforms
- most deposition takes place in the river's lower course;
- features formed by deposition include floodplains, deltas and levées;
- meanders and ox-bow lakes are formed as a result of both erosion and deposition;
- the valley cross-section changes to a broad U-shape in the lower course;
- overall the long profile of a river is smooth and concave with a steep gradient at the source which decreases to almost nil near the river mouth.

Hints and Tips!

An easy way to remember these processes is with the acronym – **HACC**.
Hydraulic action
Attrition
Corrasion
Corrosion
Always include these processes every time a question asks you to explain a landform of erosion.

Cover up the definitions and describe the four processes of erosion and transportation.

Key words and definitions

Fluvial processes

Erosion	Transportation	Deposition
Hydraulic power – the force of the water eroding the bed and banks	Traction – boulders rolling along the river bed	The laying down of material by the river
Attrition – the load rubbing against each other becoming smaller and more rounded	Saltation – small particles 'jumping' along the river bed	
Corrasion – or abrasion, the wearing away of the river banks by the load carried in the river	Solution – material carried along dissolved in the water	
Corrosion – the chemical action of water dissolving minerals	Suspension – small particles of clay, silt carried along in the river flow	

Landforms

Erosion	Deposition	Erosion and deposition
Gorge of recession – steep sided narrow valley created by waterfall retreat	Delta – often triangular shaped flat land jutting out into the sea at the mouth of a river.	Meanders – bends in the middle and lower course of a river
Waterfall – a high head of water along a stretch of river	Flood plain – the flat, low lying valley floor adjacent to a river in its lower course	Ox-bow lakes – semi-circular lakes formed by sealing off a meander bend
	Levées – high mounds of silt on the river banks, formed by flooding	

Hints and Tips!

Read examination questions carefully.

Does the question ask about the river channel, the river valley, or both?

Remember the channel is only the part in which the river flows.

The valley includes the land either side of the river too.

River basins

Rivers begin in upland areas and flow downhill, becoming wider and deeper until they enter the sea. Figure 1 shows a typical drainage basin of a river. A drainage basin is part of the hydrological cycle in which water is recycled between the sea, the atmosphere and the land.

As the river flows downstream the characteristics of the channel and the river valley change. Changes along a river valley allow it to be subdivided into three sections:
- the upper course
- the middle course
- the lower course.

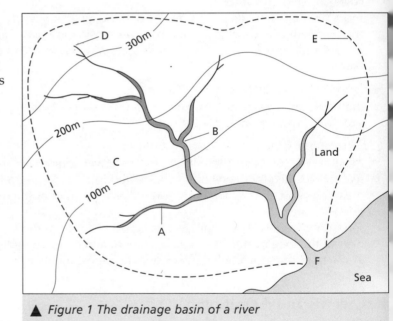

▲ *Figure 1 The drainage basin of a river*

Test Yourself

A   Tops and tails – match the correct word to the following definitions:

Tributary   Confluence   Mouth   Watershed   Source   Drainage basin

_____ :   where two rivers meet

_____ :   the area drained by a river and its tributaries

_____ :   where a river flows into the sea

_____ :   where the river begins

_____ :   a smaller river which flows into a larger river

_____ :   the imaginary line surrounding a drainage basin

If your answers are in alphabetical order you have got it all right – well done.

B   Match these labels with the correct letter on Figure 1:

Tributary   Confluence   Mouth   Watershed   Source   Drainage basin

The upper course of a river

In the upper course, the river is high above its base level (usually sea level). This gives the river a lot of potential energy. The river is trying to cut down to its base level so it mainly erodes in a downwards direction (vertical erosion). This helps to create the V-shaped river valleys in upland areas.

Landforms in the upper course

1   The river valley
In the upper course the river valley is often V-shaped with interlocking spurs as shown in Figure 2.

2   The river channel
The main characteristics of the channel in the upper course are:
- it is narrow and shallow with large angular boulders
- the channel has a steep gradient especially at rapids and waterfalls where the velocity of the water is also high
- there is a low velocity in most stretches because so much energy is lost overcoming friction with the bed and banks
- the water is often clear because there has been very little abrasion and attrition so the suspended load is very small.

3   Waterfalls and gorges (Figure 3)
Characteristics of waterfalls:
- a steep drop in the course of the river
- plunge pool at the base
- a hard, resistant cap rock at the top of the waterfall which often overhangs
- softer rocks which are undercut
- waterfall often lies in a steep-sided gorge.

Formation
Figure 3 shows how a waterfall is formed. There is a band of resistant rock between softer rocks. The less resistant rock erodes more quickly by the processes of erosion. Remember **HACC** – **h**ydraulic power, **a**ttrition, **c**orrosion and **c**orrasion. The hard rock is undercut and overhangs until it eventually collapses. Gradually the waterfall retreats upstream forming a gorge of recession. The great power of the waterfall moves material at the base to form a deep plunge pool.

Figure 2 V-shaped valley with interlocking spurs

Labels on Figure 2: V-shaped valley, Interlocking spurs, Narrow winding river

DID YOU KNOW?

The highest waterfalls in the world are the Angel Falls in Venezuela.

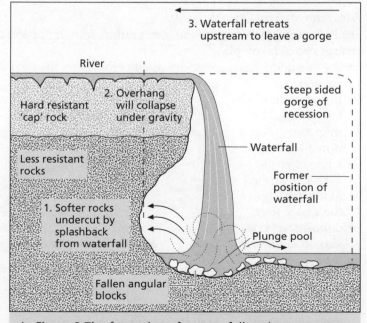

▲ *Figure 3 The formation of a waterfall and gorge*

Labels on Figure 3: River; Hard resistant 'cap' rock; Less resistant rocks; 2. Overhang will collapse under gravity; 1. Softer rocks undercut by splashback from waterfall; Fallen angular blocks; 3. Waterfall retreats upstream to leave a gorge; Steep sided gorge of recession; Waterfall; Former position of waterfall; Plunge pool

The middle course of a river

As the river flows downstream the gradient becomes less steep. Lateral or sideways erosion becomes more important than vertical erosion and the river starts to meander. Some of the river's energy is also used to transport eroded material downstream. Figure 1 shows the four ways a river transports material.

Meanders

A meander is a bend in a river (Figure 2). As the water flows round the bend the flow is faster on the outside bend where the water is deeper. The force of the water erodes and undercuts the outside bend by corrasion

Traction–large boulders roll along the river bed

Saltation–smaller pebbles are bounced along the river bed, picked up and then dropped as the flow of the river changes

Suspension–the finer sand and silt-sized particles are carried along in the flow, giving the river a brown appearance

Solution–minerals, such as limestone and chalk, are dissolved in the water and carried along in the flow, although they cannot be seen

▲ *Figure 1 Transporting the river's load*

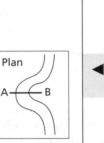

◀ *Figure 2 Cross-section through a meander*

forming a steep bank called a river cliff. The erosion on the outer bend removes the ends of the interlocking spurs widening the valley and creating a more recognisable flat valley floor. On the inside bend the water is shallow and flows more slowly which encourages deposition. Sand and pebbles are deposited forming a slip-off slope.

The material transported by a river is called the **load**.

Meander migration

Study Figure 3 showing meander migration. Moving downstream several changes have taken place:

- the meanders have got wider due to erosion on the outside bend – lateral erosion
- the meanders have moved or migrated downstream
- a line of river cliffs has formed along the edge of the valley floor
- deposition on the slip-off slopes has built up alluvium on the valley floor
- as the meanders get wider so does the valley floor or flood plain.

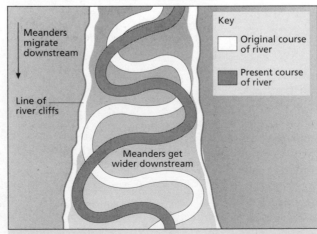

▲ *Figure 3 Meander migration*

How and why would a river's load change if:

- the river has a large volume of water?
- the river's velocity is high?
- the river flows over hard, resistant rock types, e.g. granite?

The lower course of a river

The river is nearing the sea now and deposition becomes the most important process encouraged by:
- the large load carried by the river
- any obstruction, e.g. a lake, weir or bridge supports
- any fall in the volume, e.g. in the summer
- any loss of velocity, e.g. on the inside bend of a meander

Features of the channel in the lower course
- it is wide and deep, often with a semi-circular shape
- is lined with sand and mud making it smooth
- there may be islands of silt called eyots
- the river carries a large load of alluvium

Features of the valley in the lower course
- there is a wide, flat **flood plain** either side of the river
- **levées** may be found on the river banks
- there are **ox-bow lakes** and **meander scars**
- the flood plain is made up of great thicknesses of alluvium
- a **line of river cliffs** is found at the edge of the flood plain

Test Yourself

On Figure 4, label the five features in **bold** type in the text.

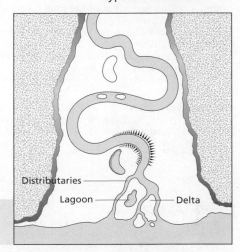

Distributaries

Lagoon ——— Delta

▶ *Figure 4 Features of the flood plain*

Ox-bow lakes

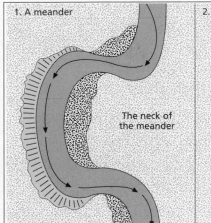

1. A meander

The neck of the meander

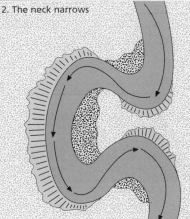

2. The neck narrows

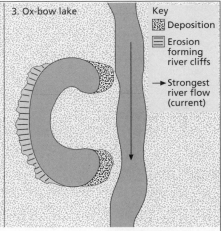

3. Ox-bow lake

Key

▨ Deposition

☰ Erosion forming river cliffs

→ Strongest river flow (current)

The meander becomes even larger in the lower course. Erosion by corrasion and hydraulic power continues on the outer bends and deposition on the slip–off slopes.

The erosion causes the meander neck to narrow until eventually it is broken through. This often happens during a flood when the river has extra energy.

The river now follows a straight path. After the flood, the meander is sealed off by deposition of alluvium to form an ox-bow lake. Gradually the lake may dry up to form a meander scar.

▲ *Figure 5 Formation of an ox-bow lake*

The flood plain

The flood plain is the wide, flat area of land either side of the river in its lower course. It is formed by both erosion and deposition:
- erosion increases the width of the flood plain. The meanders erode laterally and migrate downstream widening the flood plain.
- deposition increases the depth of silt on the flood plain. Deposition on the slip-off slopes and in times of flood, build up the alluvium on the flood plain

Test Yourself

Cover up this page. Practice drawing and labelling the diagrams to show the formation of an ox-bow lake. Explain how an ox-bow lake and the flood plain are formed.

Levées

Levées are natural embankments of silt along the banks of rivers. Large sections of the Mississippi river have natural levées. Levées are formed along rivers that:

- flow slowly,
- carry a large load
- flood from time to time.

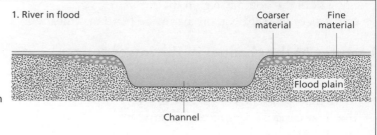

▼ *Figure 1 The formation of levées*

1 River in flood

When the river floods the water leaves the channel and immediately slows down. It loses energy and so must deposit the load it is carrying. It deposits the coarser, heavier material on the river bank and finer material further away. The river bank is also covered by water for longer so there is more deposition which builds up a narrow bank.

2 River at low flow

At times of low flow the river's velocity slows down and load is deposited. The river bed is raised by the deposits.

3 After repeated floods

After many floods the river banks are built up to form levées. The river bed may also be raised so much that the river is now above the level of the flood plain. This can lead to catastrophic flooding because the water cannot drain back into the river.

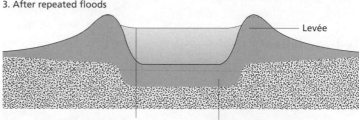

The river mouth

As a river reaches the sea there may be a delta or an estuary.

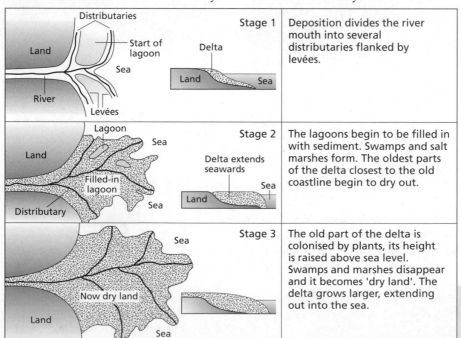

Stage 1	Deposition divides the river mouth into several distributaries flanked by levées.
Stage 2	The lagoons begin to be filled in with sediment. Swamps and salt marshes form. The oldest parts of the delta closest to the old coastline begin to dry out.
Stage 3	The old part of the delta is colonised by plants, its height is raised above sea level. Swamps and marshes disappear and it becomes 'dry land'. The delta grows larger, extending out into the sea.

◀ *Figure 2 Stages in the formation of a delta (after Bunnett)*

Hints and Tips!

Examination questions often ask 'Describe the physical features of, for example, a delta' or 'Explain the formation of, for example, a levée'

You can save writing time in the exam by drawing simple diagrams and labelling them accurately in order to answer the question.

Key Idea 2: Landscape features affect human activities

What you need to study and to know:
- land uses in an upland river basin in the UK include forestry, dams and sheep farming;
- land uses in lowland river basins in the UK are more urban, e.g. cities and ports in estuaries;
- it is sometimes desirable to manage river basins in order to reduce the impact of flooding and to provide a water supply;
- river measurements are used to draw hydrographs which show how a river responds to heavy rainfall;
- the main causes of flooding are natural such as heavy rain and snow melt. River flooding can lead to loss of life, property and animals;
- people have tried to prevent river flooding by a variety of methods including dam building, raising levées and straightening rivers.

Study Figure 3.

Where is the source of the River Tees?

Where is the mouth of the River Tees?

Name one town at a confluence.

In which direction does the River Tees flow?

Know your case study

Land uses in the Tees river basin
Location: north-east England

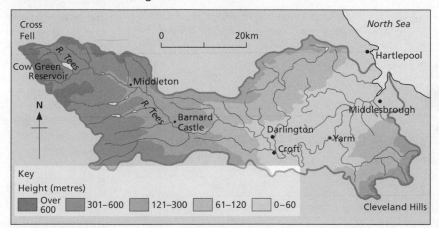

◄ *Figure 3 The drainage basin of the River Tees*

Characteristics of the river Tees and its valley in the uplands
- Source high up at 893 metres above sea level with high rainfall, over 2000 millimetres a year
- Steep-sided, V-shaped valley with a steep gradient
- Clear and turbulent river with a rocky river bed
- A waterfall and gorge at High Force and rapids at Low Force

Land uses and human activity in the uplands
Communications and building settlements are difficult on the steep slopes. Employment opportunities are limited to sheep farming, the water industry, forestry, quarrying and tourism. The population density is low and most settlements are found alongside the roads and on the lower valley sides.

Land uses and human activity in the lowlands of the River Tees
In the lowlands the river and its valley changes; the valley is wider and flatter, the river meanders in broad loops. At the river mouth there is a large estuary with mud flats which is an ideal site for large industries, such as chemicals and steel, and large urban areas, such as Middlesbrough and Billingham. The River Tees has many examples of basin management. There are reservoirs in the upper course, and flood defence schemes at Yarm and Stockton which include the Tees Barrage, cut-offs and flood warning systems.

Hints and Tips!

Make sure you know your case studies of an upland drainage basin and lowland drainage basin. You need to be able to describe and explain the land uses. Remember the best answers in an examination will include accurately used place names and other real facts.

Flooding and flood hydrographs

Flooding is a normal occurrence in the lower course of a river. It occurs when the river overflows its banks and leaves the channel. River flooding helps to form several river features: flood plains, ox-bow lakes and levées.

Causes of flooding

Natural
- Long, continuous rainfall
- Cloud-burst in a thunderstorm
- Rapid melting of snow and ice

Human
- Expanding urban areas
- Deforestation
- Occasional disasters, e.g. dam burst

Flood hydrographs

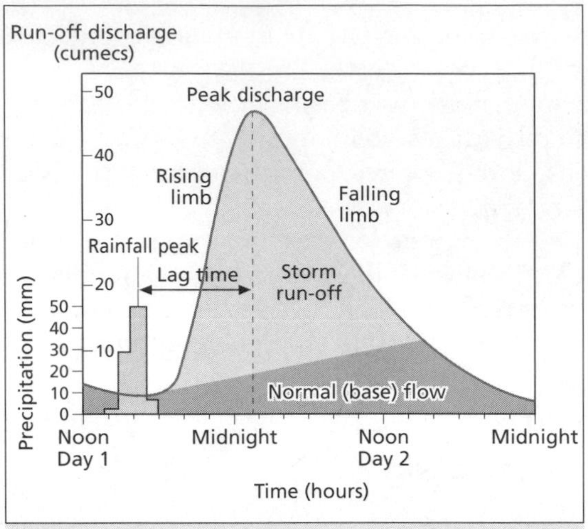

▲ Figure 1 A flood hydrograph showing the discharge of a river over a period of time

1 Read each of the causes of flooding carefully. Can you explain how each one would cause river flooding?

2 Which of the following statements would be more likely to cause high runoff and flooding in a river basin?

i) A long period of light rain *or* a short heavy thunderstorm

ii) A basin with steep valley slopes *or* a basin with gentle slopes

iii) A basin with a large expanse of forest *or* a basin with moorland and few trees

iv) A mainly urbanized basin *or* a mainly rural basin

v) A basin with a large dam and reservoir *or* a basin with no reservoir or dam

Know your case study

The Mississippi Floods

In 1993, the Mississippi river caused the worst flooding in the USA since records began. The floods were caused by snow melt and 50 days of very heavy rain. The effects of the floods were:
- 28 lives lost
- 36 000 people made homeless and many more evacuated
- roads and railways under water
- electricity lines collapsed
- six million acres of farmland flooded, maize crops ruined
- US$10 billion needed to repair flood damage

Flood protection

Protecting against floods can be achieved in different ways:
1 Reduce the impact of flooding by early warning systems and zoning the land uses on a flood plain.
2 Try to stop the river flooding, e.g. by building dams, raising levées, planting trees, dredging, straightening the river.

Examination practice question

(a) (i)   Describe the appearance of a waterfall.   (2 marks)

     (ii) Using one or more diagrams, explain the formation of a waterfall.   (6 marks)

(b) (i)   Name one technique used to prevent flooding.   (1 mark)

     (ii) Explain how the technique you chose in (b) (i) would help to prevent flooding.   (2 marks)

     (iii) Using a case study of a flood, describe the causes and effects of the flooding in the area affected.   (4 marks)

[Check your answers on page 123]   Total = 15 marks

Summary

Key words from the syllabus

attrition	flood plain	meanders
corrasion	gorge	ox-bow lakes
cross profile	hydraulic power	saltation
delta	hydrograph	suspension
deposition	levées	traction
estuary	long profile	waterfall
flood		

Test Yourself

Write down a definition for each of the key words. Check them with those given on page 21.

Checklist for revision

	Understand and know	Need more revision	Do not understand	Hints and tips
I know the features of a river basin (watershed, source, mouth, confluence, drainage basin)	☐	☐	☐	pp 32-3
I know the long profile of a river and how the cross-section changes downstream	☐	☐	☐	pp 32, 33, 48
I know four processes of erosion	☐	☐	☐	p 34
I can describe and explain the formation of waterfalls and gorges	☐	☐	☐	p 35
I know four methods of transport by rivers	☐	☐	☐	p 36
I know the features and formation of meanders, ox-bow lakes, flood plains, deltas and levées	☐	☐	☐	pp 36-8
I understand how and why a river deposits its load	☐	☐	☐	p 37

Hints and Tips!

The page numbers refer to where the topic can be found in your text book *Understanding GCSE Geography*. If you don't understand the topic, read the relevant section in your text book, make some notes and learn about it.

Test Yourself

Tick the boxes and fill in the gaps – if you still do not understand seek help from your teacher.

Know your case studies

Which real places have you studied as an example of...

- a waterfall and gorge   name:_____ p 40
- meanders and ox-bow lakes   name:_____ p 42
- a flood plain   name:_____ p 42
- a delta   name:_____ p 39
- land uses in an upland river basin   name:_____ pp 40-1
- land uses in an estuary   name:_____ p 42
- river flooding   name:_____ pp 46-7
- water supply   name:_____ p 41

4 Ice

> **Key Ideas**
> 1 The action of glaciation produces distinctive landforms.
> 2 Landscape features affect human actvities.
> Each key idea will be looked at in turn.

Exam Watch

A question on this topic appears in Section B in your first written paper.

It is a 15 mark question and it will be Question 7.

Key words and definitions

abrasion	rocks carried by the ice are used to erode the rock below
arête	sharp-edged, two-sided ridge on the top of a mountain
boulder clay	materials deposited by ice usually unsorted clay and boulders
corrie	circular, steep-sided rocky hollow high on a mountain side
drumlins	egg shaped hills of boulder clay
ice sheet	a moving mass of ice which covers a wide area
glacial trough	flat-floored and steep-sided U-shaped valley
hanging valley	a waterfall from a tributary valley left high above the main valley
moraine	all materials deposited after having been transported by ice
plucking	erosion by blocks of rock being torn away as the ice moves
pyramidal peak	three-sided slab of rock which forms a mountain peak
ribbon lake	long and narrow lake in the floor of a glaciated valley
till (glacial)	all materials deposited by ice; an alternative term for boulder clay
truncated spurs	higher areas on the straight rocky sides of the glaciated valley
valley glacier	a moving mass of ice confined within a valley

Key Idea 1: the action of glaciation produces distinctive landforms

What you need to study and to know:

A Ice erosion and the resulting landforms:
- processes of ice erosion are abrasion and plucking;
- freeze-thaw weathering helps to produce landforms of ice erosion as well;
- the distinctive landforms formed are arêtes and pyramidal peaks, corries, and glacial troughs which are U-shaped valleys with hanging valleys, truncated spurs and ribbon lakes.

B Transport of materials by the ice:
- glaciers transport boulders and loose materials on the surface, in the middle and at the bottom of the ice.

C Ice deposition and resulting landforms:
- most of the deposition occurs on the valley floor and in the lowlands where the ice melts;
- the distinctive landforms produced by ice deposition are drumlins and different types of moraines (such as terminal moraines and lateral moraines).

Test Yourself

Put a piece of paper over the definitions or the key words.

See if you can remember them.

A Ice erosion and the resulting landforms

There are two processes of ice erosion, which wear away the rocks over which the glaciers flow.

- Abrasion – the sharp-edged rocks carried in the bottom of the glacier are used like files to wear away the rock below the ice.
- Plucking – blocks of rock are torn away from surface rocks by the moving ice.

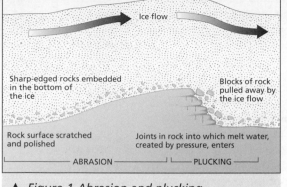

Figure 1 Abrasion and plucking

Freeze-thaw weathering greatly helps the work of ice erosion because
(a) water seeps into joints in the rock; when it freezes it expands and helps to break off pieces of rock;
(b) the loose pieces of rock broken off by freeze-thaw can be picked up by the glaciers and used as tools for abrasion.

Landforms of ice erosion

Corries, arêtes and pyramidal peaks: these are shown and described by labels in Figure 2.

Formation of corries

- snow collects on a mountain side and is compressed into ice
- freeze-thaw weathering affects the back of the hollow and makes it steeper
- blocks of rock are pulled away from the back wall by plucking
- the glacier uses the loose rocks to scrape out the bottom of the hollow by abrasion
- the greatest pressure from the ice is at the bottom of the back wall because of the rotational slip movement
- this results in a deep hollow, with a steep back wall and a rock lip at the front

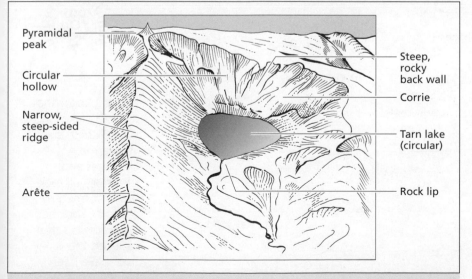

◄ *Figure 2 Corries, arêtes and pyramidal peaks*

Abrasion and plucking are examples of processes.

Processes are responsible for changes and for making something happen.

Hints and Tips!
Refer to abrasion and plucking every time you are asked to explain the formation of a landform of glacial erosion.

What is freeze-thaw?

If you don't know, look back at page 15.

Hints and Tips!
The labels on Figure 2 describe the features.

Draw a quick sketch of Figure 2.

Add labels for the formation of a corrie.

The corrie was the first landform to be formed by the glacier. Once you understand corrie formation, it is easier to understand the formation of other landforms such as arêtes, pyramidal peaks and tarn lakes.

Formation of arêtes

An arête is the sharp, knife-edged ridge at the top of a mountain between two corries. As the back wall of each corrie is cut back by weathering and erosion, the ridge between them (i.e. the arête) becomes narrower and sharper. Therefore to explain the formation of an arête, use the same points made on page 31 for corrie formation, emphasizing the formation of the steep back wall. Then finish off your answer by adding comments specific to the arête:

- as the back walls of two corries are cut back, only a narrow ridge is left between them
- this ridge is kept sharp by freeze-thaw on the mountain peaks.

Glaciated valley landforms

Valley glaciers change small, V-shaped river valleys into large U-shaped glaciated valleys, called glacial troughs, with flat floors, steep rocky valley slopes, straight sides lined by waterfalls (hanging valleys) and uneven floors. Glaciers can do this because:

- glaciers are much bigger and heavier than rivers and have more power to erode;
- glaciers fill the whole of the valley bottom so that they erode all the floor and the sides of the valley as well;
- glaciers have the weight and power to flow straight down the valley.

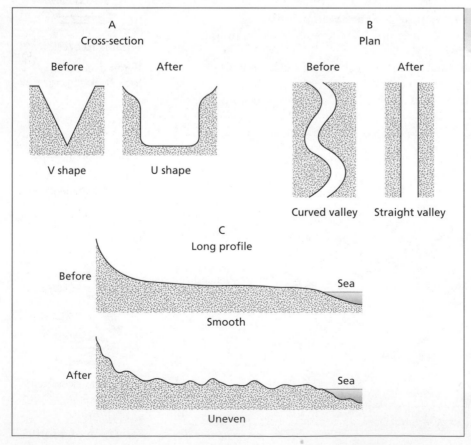

A
Cross-section

Before   After

V shape   U shape

B
Plan

Before   After

Curved valley   Straight valley

C
Long profile

Before   Sea

Smooth

After   Sea

Uneven

◄ Figure 1 River valleys changed by glaciers

Hints and Tips!

Make sure that you can name an actual example of a corrie, arête, pyramidal peak and tarn lake.

Write them down now.

Write down notes for the formation of a tarn lake.

You need to explain the formation of the corrie hollow first.

Then you need to explain why water will be trapped in it.

Check that you can explain how abrasion and plucking help to form a U-shaped valley.

Did you know that all the large lakes in the Lake District, such as Windermere, Ullswater and Coniston, fill rock basins formed by ice erosion? Rock basins form where softer rocks on the valley floor have been eroded most by glaciers.

B Ice transport

Most of the rocks and smaller materials eroded by the glaciers are carried in the bottom of the ice. This forms the ground moraine. Some material is carried at the sides of the glacier, which is called lateral moraine. If it is carried in the middle of the glacier, it is called medial moraine. Where the ice melts there is a terminal moraine.

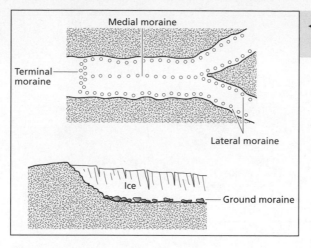

◀ *Figure 2 The four types of moraine*

Test Yourself

Cover up the diagram.

Practise drawing and naming the four types of moraine.

C Ice deposition

Where does it take place? – On valley floors and in the lowlands.

When does it occur? – As the ice thins and melts.

Why does it happen? – The glacier carries less when temperatures increase.

Landforms which result from ice deposition

All are made of boulder clay. Boulder clay is an unsorted mixture of everything that was carried by glaciers – boulders, stones, clay and sand.

Drumlins are formed when the ice is still moving fast enough for the boulder clay to be moulded into shape. Moraines are formed when the ice cannot carry the boulder clay any further and it is just dumped. More tends to be dumped at the end of the glacier than along its sides which is why the terminal moraine is usually larger than lateral moraines.

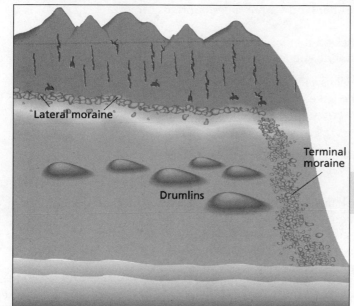

◀ *Figure 3 Landforms of glacial deposition*

DID YOU KNOW?

There is no boulder clay in counties in southern England which border the English Channel. The ice didn't reach that far.

Formation of a terminal moraine

- The glacier carries a large load of materials from erosion and weathering
- All the ice is melting at the snout because of high temperatures
- The load is dropped and dumped because it cannot be transported any further
- A ridge of boulder clay is built up across the low ground
- The longer the glacier stops in the same position, the higher the ridge becomes

DID YOU KNOW?

Most ribbon lakes are formed by ice erosion. However, some are formed by ice deposition. The terminal moraine can act like a dam. It traps water behind it in a ribbon lake.

Key Idea 2: landscape features affect human activities

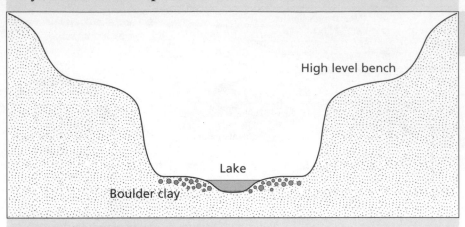

Figure 1 Glaciated upland area

Which labels would you add to Figure 1 if you were answering a question about farming?

Which labels would you use for a tourist question?

What you need to study and to know:

Opportunities for farming

The flat land on the valley floor can be used by farmers for growing crops, making hay and keeping animals there in winter. The advantages of the valley floor for farming include:

- greater thickness of soil as a result of glacial deposition
- some boulder clay soils are fertile and good for grass growth
- it is often the only area of flat land within the mountains for crop growing
- it is easier to use machines on the flat land
- the steep valley sides provide shelter.

The fells and high-level benches can be used as summer pastures for animals, mainly sheep in the Lake District and cattle in the Alps. This allows the land around the farm on the valley floor to be used for crops and hay.

Opportunities for tourism

Upland areas which have been glaciated offer many attractions for tourists. These include:

- steep mountains and rock faces for mountaineering and climbing
- rugged scenery for hiking and fell walking
- glaciers and steep slopes covered by snow in winter for skiing
- high-level benches for locating ski resorts
- lakes for sailing and water-skiing
- dramatic scenery, including waterfalls, for sightseeing.

Figure 2 shows some of the conflicts which arise between farmers and tourists. Why do conflicts like these arise?

What can be done to reduce these conflicts?

How can some farmers make money out of tourist visitors?

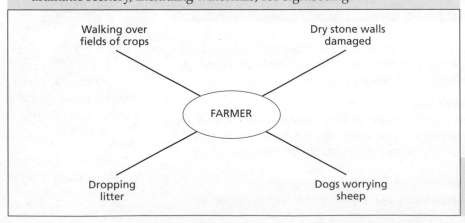

Figure 2 Conflicts between farmers and tourists

Management of tourists in glaciated upland areas

Management has two aims:

Reduce damage to the environment

There is a great risk of erosion from people walking or skiing in upland areas. The soil is thin and there is often little vegetation cover to hold the soil together. People's boots or skis soon loosen the soil which is washed away down the steep slopes.

Possible management strategies:
- change the courses of footpaths or use different slopes for skiing;
- give the vegetation time to recover on the paths and ski slopes;
- make some artificial surfaces.

Reduce conflicts between
(a) tourists and farmers;
(b) between tourists with different interests.

Possible management strategies:
- keep the different groups as separate as possible;
- educate people about the needs of other groups.

Hints and Tips!

Make sure you know a case study of a glaciated upland area, such as the Lake District.

For this area, give a named example of:
- an arête;
- a corrie with tarn lake;
- a ribbon lake;
- a U-shaped valley.

Make notes for a case study of an area within it, such as around Lake Windermere.

Mention:
- reasons for the formation of the lake;
- what visitors come to the lake to do;
- visitor conflicts and attempts to manage them.

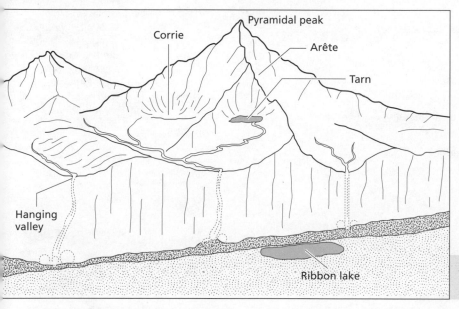

◀ *Figure 3 Glaciated upland area*

Examination practice question

(a) Look at Figure 3 which shows landforms in an upland area which has been glaciated. State the differences between:

   (i) a pyramidal peak and an arête;   (2 marks)

   (ii) a tarn lake and a ribbon lake.   (2 marks)

(b) Explain how an arête is formed.   (4 marks)

(c) Why do some glaciated uplands attract tourist visitors?   (3 marks)

(d) (i) Name one problem or conflict which is caused by tourists visiting a glaciated upland area.   (1 mark)

   (ii) Explain why it occurs and what can be done to reduce its effects.   (3 marks)

[Check your answers on pages 123-4]   Total: 15 marks

Summary

Key words from the syllabus

abrasion (glacial)	ice sheet	pyramidal peak
arête	glacial trough	ribbon lake
boulder clay	hanging valley	till (glacial)
corrie	moraine	truncated spurs
drumlins	plucking	valley glacier

Checklist for revision

	Understand and know	Need more revision	Do not understand	Hints and tips
I can name the two processes of glacial erosion	☐	☐	☐	p 50
I understand why valley glaciers have great powers of erosion	☐	☐	☐	p 51
I understand the formation of a corrie	☐	☐	☐	pp 52-3
I know the similarities and differences between an arête and a pyramidal peak	☐	☐	☐	p 53
I can describe the main features of a glaciated valley	☐	☐	☐	p 54
I understand the formation of a glacial trough (U-shaped valley)	☐	☐	☐	pp 54-5
I can explain why glaciers and ice sheets deposit their load	☐	☐	☐	p 56
I can describe the features of boulder clay deposits	☐	☐	☐	p 56
I can name the four types of glacial moraine	☐	☐	☐	p 56-7
I know the features and formation of drumlins	☐	☐	☐	p 57
I can explain two different ways for the formation of ribbon lakes	☐	☐	☐	pp 55, 57
I can describe the main features of farming in upland areas which have been glaciated	☐	☐	☐	p 58
I know some of the advantages and disadvantages of tourism in glaciated upland areas	☐	☐	☐	pp 59, 60

Test Yourself

Write down a definition for each of the key words. Check them with those given on page 30.

Hints and Tips!

The page numbers refer to where the topic can be found in your text book *Understanding GCSE Geography*. If you don't understand the topic read the relevant section in your text book, make some notes and learn about it.

Test Yourself

Tick the boxes and fill in the gaps – if you still do not understand seek help from your teacher.

Know your case studies

Which real places have you studied as an example of...
- a corrie and related features   name:_____ pp 52-3
- a glaciated valley   name:_____ p 55
- human activities in a glaciated area   name:_____ pp 59, 60

5 Coasts

Key Ideas
1 Coastal processes produce distinctive landforms.
2 Landscape features affect human activities.
Each key idea will be looked at in turn.

A question on this topic appears in Section B in your first written paper.

It is a 15 mark question and it will be Question 8.

Key words and definitions

arch	an opening through a headland
attrition	erosion by which pebbles are reduced in size
beach	a gently sloping area of sand and shingle along the edge of the sea
cave	a hollowed out area at the bottom of a cliff
cliff	a rock face, often vertical, next to the sea
constructive wave	a low wave which encourages deposition of beach materials
corrasion	erosion by pebbles thrown against the cliff face by waves
corrosion	erosion caused by some rocks being dissolved by chemical action
destructive wave	a high wave which breaks frequently causing erosion
hydraulic power	erosion caused by the weight and force of the water
spit	a long narrow ridge of sand and shingle ending in the open sea
stack	a piece of rock, surrounded by sea, left standing away from the coastline
wave cut platform	a gently sloping area of flat rocks which is exposed at low tide

Key Idea 1: coastal processes produce distinctive landforms
What you need to study and to know:

A Coastal erosion and the resulting landforms
- processes of coastal erosion are hydraulic action, attrition, corrasion and corrosion;
- most erosion is done by destructive waves;
- the distinctive landforms formed by coastal erosion are cliffs, wave cut platforms, caves, stacks and arches.

B Transport of materials by the waves
- longshore drift transports materials along the coast;
- currents pick up eroded materials and deposit them further along the coast.

C Coastal deposition and resulting landforms
- coastal deposition is done by constructive waves;
- the distinctive landforms formed by coastal deposition are beaches and spits.

Put a piece of paper over the definitions or the names.

See if you can remember them.

Looking at what you need to know and study in more detail

A Coastal erosion and the resulting landforms

Processes of coastal erosion are those which do the work of wearing away the rocks along the coast. There are four processes of coastal erosion.

- **Hydraulic power** – force of the water and weight of the waves against the rocks
- **Attrition** – breaking down boulders and pebbles into something smaller such as sand
- **Corrasion** – pieces of rock broken off by waves and thrown against the rock face
- **Corrosion** – chemical action changing limestone and chalk rocks into solution

Hints and Tips!

Memory aid: remember **HACC** for the processes of erosion.

Hydraulic action
Attrition
Corrasion
Corrosion

Refer to these processes of erosion every time a question asks you to explain a landform of erosion.

The processes of erosion are carried out by destructive waves. The characteristics of destructive waves are:

- high waves
- with a strong backwash
- breaking frequently between 11 and 15 times per minute.

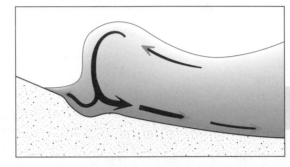

◀ *Figure 1 A destructive wave*

Can you explain why some coasts are being eroded more quickly than others?

Landforms of coastal erosion

1 Cliffs and wave cut platforms

These are shown and described by labels on Figure 2.

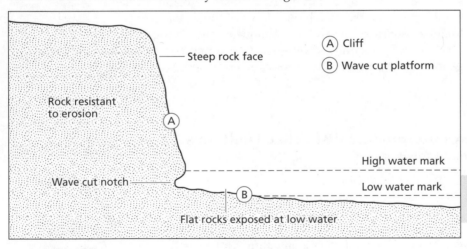

Ⓐ Cliff
Ⓑ Wave cut platform

Steep rock face

Rock resistant to erosion

High water mark

Low water mark

Wave cut notch

Flat rocks exposed at low water

Hints and Tips!

The labels on Figure 2 describe the features

◀ *Figure 2 Cliffs and wave cut platform*

Formation of cliffs

- bottom of rock face attacked by destructive waves
- eroded by hydraulic action, attrition, corrasion and corrosion
- waves undercut the rock face to form a notch
- the overhanging rock collapses
- this happens many times and the cliff retreats inland

Formation of wave cut platforms

Begin by explaining the formation of a cliff; make the same five points listed above. Then add the following two points.

- as the cliff retreats inland an area of flat rock is left which is exposed at low tide
- the rock above has been eroded away by the waves

1   Practise drawing a sketch of a destructive wave. Label its characteristics.

2   Draw your own sketch of Figure 2. Add labels for the formation of cliffs.

2 Caves, arches and stacks

A cave forms first, which may then become an arch and finally a stack. What is needed for a cave to form is a line of weakness in the rock, such as a joint, which destructive waves can erode away more quickly than the rock on either side of it. The line of weakness is widened by destructive waves and the processes of erosion (**H**ydraulic action, **A**ttrition, **C**orrasion and **C**orrosion). The weak point in the rock is first hollowed out into a cave. The back of the cave is eroded backwards through to the other side of the headland, when a hole through the rock makes an arch. Further erosion leads to the collapse of the roof of the arch and this forms the stack.

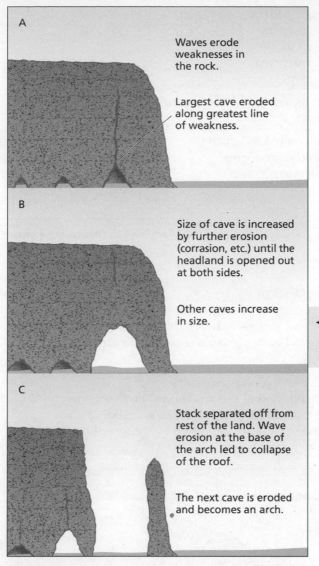

A Waves erode weaknesses in the rock.

Largest cave eroded along greatest line of weakness.

B Size of cave is increased by further erosion (corrasion, etc.) until the headland is opened out at both sides.

Other caves increase in size.

C Stack separated off from rest of the land. Wave erosion at the base of the arch led to collapse of the roof.

The next cave is eroded and becomes an arch.

◀ *Figure 3 Formation of caves, arches and stacks*

B Transport of materials by the waves

Eroded materials are moved along the coast by longshore drift. The drift is pushed along a coast by the dominant wind. Waves may carry sand and pebbles up the beach at an angle but they always roll back down the beach at right angles to the coastline. This gives the zig-zag movement of sand and pebbles along the coast.

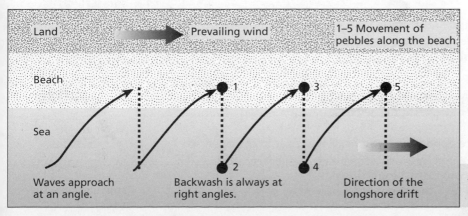

Land   Prevailing wind   1–5 Movement of pebbles along the beach

Beach

Sea

Waves approach at an angle.

Backwash is always at right angles.

Direction of the longshore drift

◀ *Figure 4 Longshore drift*

Hints and Tips!

Make sure that you can name an example of a cave, an arch and a stack.

Write them down now.

Do the same for a cliff and a wave cut platform.

Longshore drift moves from west to east along the Channel coast.

Longshore drift moves from north to south down the east coast of Britain.

Hints and Tips!

When you draw a diagram to show longshore drift, make sure that you show the movement back down the beach at right angles to the coastline.

C Coastal deposition and resulting landforms

This occurs where conditions are favourable for longshore drift to deposit the sand and pebbles which are being transported.

Good places for deposition are:
- in a sheltered spot such as in a bay;
- on a bend in the coastline.

Constructive waves deposit materials which form landforms such as beaches and spits. The characteristics of constructive waves are:
- long, low waves
- with a weak backwash
- breaking gently between 6 and 9 times per minute.

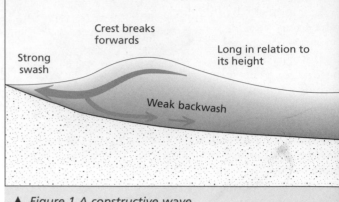

▲ *Figure 1 A constructive wave*

Landforms of coastal deposition

1 Beaches

These are the areas of sand and shingle between the high and low water marks without which you can't have a good seaside holiday resort.

Formation of beaches
- sand and shingle are carried by longshore drift
- in the shelter of a bay deposition of the sand and shingle occurrs
- constructive waves are more likely to operate in the shelter of a bay
- more and more sand and shingle are deposited by the longshore drift
- in time, these build up to form a beach

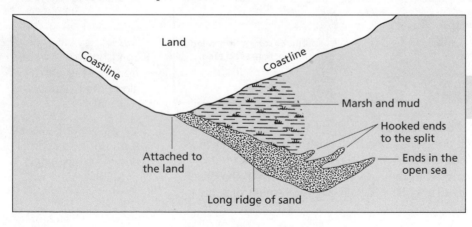

Figure 2 Features of a spit

2 Spits

These are long ridges of sand and shingle with one end attached to the land and the other ending in the open sea. One type of spit, the hooked spit, is shown and described by labels on Figure 2.

Formation of spits
- sand and shingle are carried by longshore drift
- in the shelter of a bay or at a bend in the coastline, deposition of sand and shingle occurs
- the sand and shingle are deposited away from the coast in the open sea
- more and more sand and shingle are deposited by longshore drift
- these build up with time to form a long ridge
- the edge of the long ridge in the sea may be curved by winds and currents

Test Yourself

Make a table of the differences between constructive and destructive waves.

Hints and Tips!

The labels on Figure 2 describe the spit's features.

Hints and Tips!

Notice how similar the formations of beaches and spits are. After all they are both features of coastal deposition. Only their *shapes* and *where they form* are different.

Test Yourself

Name and give the location of a spit.

Key Idea 2: landscape features affect human activities

What you need to study and to know:
- people try to keep the sea out by building defences against coastal erosion;
- seaside holiday resorts need to keep their beaches;
- by managing one part of the coastline people are likely to cause knock-on effects for another.

Sea defences against coastal erosion

The main method is to build a sea wall between the cliffs and the sea so that destructive waves can no longer reach and erode the bottom of the cliffs.

Advantages of sea walls:
- an effective method of sea defence
- safe to build on the land behind them.

Disadvantages of sea walls:
- expensive to build
- costly to maintain
- can only be used for short stretches of coast.

Another method is to build groynes up and down the beach – see below.

Keeping the beach by building groynes

Groynes are erected in parallel lines; they are usually made of wooden boards built out into the sea at right angles to the coastline. They trap the sand and shingle as it is transported along the coast by longshore drift. In this way the width of beach for tourists to use is increased. It also helps stop the waves reaching and eroding the bottom of the cliffs behind the beach.

You can work out the direction of longshore drift from groynes.

It is from north to south in Figure 3.

The evidence for this is where the sand is piling up.

You can also work out the direction of longshore drift from spits.

Note the direction of the spit out from the coastline.

Along the Channel coast spits build up from west to east.

The direction of the longshore drift is from west to east as well.

Make sure you know a case study of a managed stretch of coastline.

Mention:
- methods of sea defence;
- why defences were needed;
- their advantages and disadvantages.

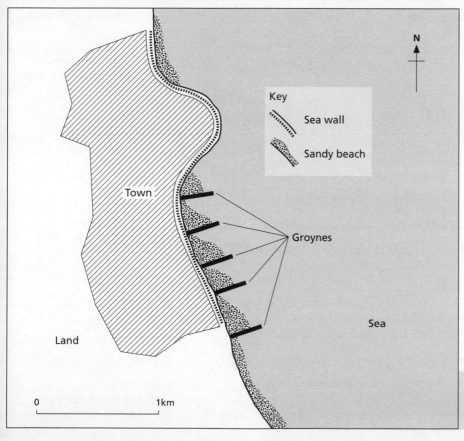

Figure 3 Coastal management methods in a seaside resort

Knock-on effects further along the coast from coastal management
Groynes and other structures built into the sea, such as breakwaters and
harbour walls, deprive the waves of their load of sand and shingle.

The consequences of this for other parts of the coastline are:

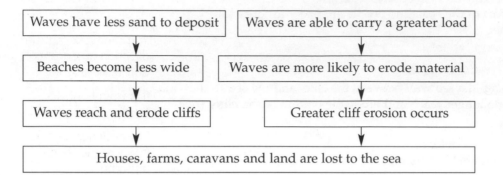

Make sure that you
know a case study
where coastal
management has
made the erosion
further along the
coast worse, such as
Holderness or Barton
on Sea.

Examination practice question

(a) (i) State two characteristic features of a destructive wave.   (2 marks)

   (ii) Explain how destructive waves help to form cliffs.   (4 marks)

(b) Figures 1A and 1B show the coastline at Beachy Head before and after a storm in January 1999.

   (i) Add labels to Figure 1B to describe the changes caused by the storm.   (3 marks)

   (ii) What are the disadvantages and dangers for people of the changes caused by
        storms, such as those shown for Beachy Head?   (3 marks)

(c) (i) Name one way of protecting a coastline against further erosion.   (1 mark)

   (ii) Why would it have been difficult to protect the coastline at Beachy Head?   (2 marks)

[Check your answers on page 124]   Total: 15 marks

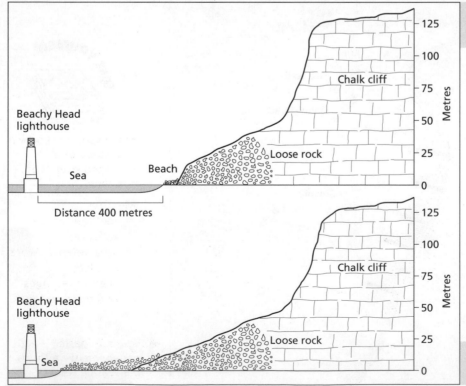

◀ *Figure 1A Beachy
Head before the storm*

◀ *Figure 1B Beachy
Head after the storm*

Summary

Key words from the syllabus		
arch	cliff	destructive wave
attrition	constructive wave	hydraulic power
beach	corrasion	spit
cave	corrosion	stack

Checklist for revision

	Understand and know	Need more revision	Do not understand	Hints and tips
I know the characteristics of destructive waves	☐	☐	☐	p 62
I can name the four processes of erosion	☐	☐	☐	p 63
I can explain how cliffs are formed	☐	☐	☐	p 64
I can give two reasons why some cliffs are being quickly eroded	☐	☐	☐	p 63
I can recognize a stack and understand its formation	☐	☐	☐	p 65
I can explain how longshore drift works	☐	☐	☐	p 66
I understand the differences between constructive and destructive waves	☐	☐	☐	pp 62, 66
I know where and why beaches form	☐	☐	☐	p 67
I can describe what a spit looks like	☐	☐	☐	p 67
I understand how a spit forms	☐	☐	☐	p 67
I can name and describe two types of coastal defences	☐	☐	☐	pp 68-9
I can give the advantages and disadvantages of coastal defences	☐	☐	☐	pp 68-9

Test Yourself

Write down a definition for each of the key words. Check them with those given on page 37.

Hints and Tips!

The page numbers refer to where the topic can be found in your text book *Understanding GCSE Geography*. If you don't understand the topic read the relevant section in your text book, make some notes and learn about it.

Test Yourself

Tick the boxes and fill in the gaps – if you still do not understand seek help from your teacher.

Know your case studies

Which real places have you studied as an example of...
- a coastline which is being rapidly eroded   name:_____ p 72
- landforms of erosion, such as caves and stacks   name:_____ p 71
- a landform of deposition, such as a spit   name:_____ p 71
- coastal management   name:_____ pp 69, 73

6 Weather and climate

Key Ideas

1 The weather and climate of a place are influenced by its location.

2 Weather and climate influence what people do (human activities).

Each key idea will be looked at in turn.

A question on this topic appears in Section B in your first written paper.

It is a 15 mark question and it will be Question 9.

Key words and definitions

anticyclone	an area of high pressure and sinking air, usually giving dry weather
climate	the average weather conditions at a place measured over a long time
depression	an area of low pressure and rising air, usually giving wet and windy weather
drought	absence of water, or rainfall amounts well below the expected average
fog	visibility less than 1 kilometre due to moisture in the atmosphere
precipitation	all types of moisture from the atmosphere such as rain, snow, hail and fog
prevailing winds	direction of the winds which blow most frequently at a place
synoptic chart	a map showing weather information such as pressure, wind, temperature and cloud
temperature	a measure of the heat of the atmosphere
tropical storm	very deep area of low pressure which forms over warm seas near the Equator
weather	day-to-day conditions of temperature, precipitation, cloud, sunshine and wind

Put a piece of paper over the words or the definitions.

Test yourself again after having read the chapter.

Key Idea 1: the weather and climate of a place are influenced by its location

What you need to study and to know:

A Factors which affect the world distribution of climates:
- latitude;
- distance from the sea;
- prevailing winds.

B Factors which cause regional differences in climate within the UK:
- temperature;
- precipitation.

C The different weather associated with depressions and anticyclones in the UK

What is the difference between weather and climate?

Weather is day to day conditions of temperature, precipitation, cloud, sunshine and wind.

Climate is the average of these weather conditions taken over many years.

A Factors which affect the world distribution of climates

Temperature is an important factor. There are four factors which affect the temperature of a place.

1 Latitude

In the tropics, the sun always shines from a high angle in the sky. This means its rays of light reach the Earth's surface directly and have only a small area to heat up. In temperate latitudes the sun's rays strike the Earth's surface at a lower angle and they have a larger surface area to heat up. Rates of solar heating, called insolation, are particularly low in winter in the UK.

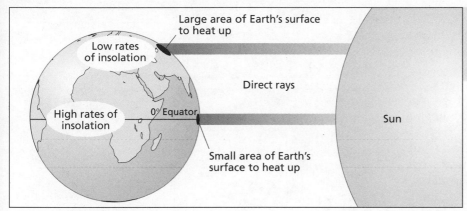

◀ Figure 1 The effects of latitude on temperature – insolation

2 Distance from the sea

Places near the sea are cooler than expected in summer because the sea surface heats up slowly. The same places are warmer than expected in winter because the sea retains its heat store longer than the land. For example, London and Warsaw are almost the same latitude so that rates of insolation should be similar, but look how different their temperatures are.

Temperature (°C)	January	July	Annual range
London (near the coast)	4	17	13
Warsaw (over 1000km inland)	−1	21	22

Hints and Tips!

Heating from the sun is called insolation.

Sol = sun (as in **sol**ar power).

Don't confuse it with insulation which means keeping the heat in.

3 Prevailing winds

Blowing from the west, these give the UK mild winters for its latitude, because they have crossed over the warmer sea and a warm ocean current, the North Atlantic Drift. A wind picks up the temperature characteristics of the surface over which it blows. That is why northerly winds blowing over the UK bring much colder weather.

4 Altitude

Temperature becomes colder with height by about 1°C for every 150 metres. Thin air means that less of the surface heat is trapped.

Precipitation is another important factor which affects climate.

The Equatorial climate is hot and wet. Air rises from hot surfaces and cools. Its moisture condenses and forms towering cumulo-nimbus clouds. The heavy downpours are an example of convectional rain. The UK's temperate maritime climate is mild and wet. It is wet because the prevailing westerly winds blow off the sea and depressions give rain along their fronts.

Test Yourself

Cover up Figure 1.

Draw your own labelled version.

Remember to keep the sun's rays the same width.

B Factors which cause regional differences in climate within the UK

The main factors are temperature and precipitation. There are three general features for the UK.

1   Temperatures in summer are highest in the south and decrease northwards (Figure 1).
    Main reason – insolation: the sun is at a higher angle in the sky in the south. Temperatures inland are higher than those near the coasts (Figure 1).
    Main reason – the darker land surface absorbs more sunlight than the sea.

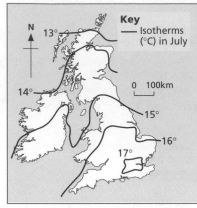

◀ *Figure 1 Summer (July) temperatures*

Hints and Tips!

Use Figure 1 on page 45 if you need to explain summer temperatures in an exam.

Isotherms link up places with the same temperature.

2   Temperatures in winter are highest in the west and decrease eastwards (Figure 2).
    Main reason – distance from the sea: the Atlantic Ocean is a lot warmer than the North Sea and continental Europe.
    Another reason – prevailing winds: westerly winds are warmed up by crossing the ocean and the warm waters of the North Atlantic Drift. They affect the west before they reach the east of the UK.

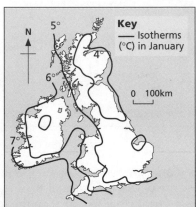

◀ *Figure 2 Winter (January) temperatures*

3   Precipitation is highest in the west and decreases eastwards (Figure 3).
    Main reason – prevailing winds: the westerly winds have had a long ocean journey and are laden with moisture when they blow onshore. Also low pressure systems approach from the west, so western areas are the first to receive rain from their fronts.

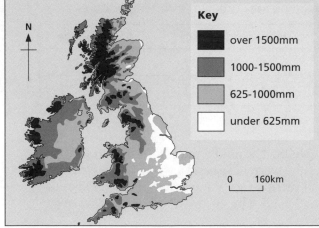

◀ *Figure 3 Average annual precipitation*

Another reason – relief: the highest land is in the west which gives relief rainfall compared with a rain shadow to the east of the hills.

If we look at the combined effects of these three general features, the UK can be split up into four regions (Figure 4).

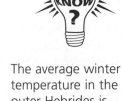

The average winter temperature in the outer Hebrides is warmer than in London.

But it is 4°C colder in summer.

◀ *Figure 4*

C Weather associated with depressions and anticyclones in the UK

Depressions are areas of low pressure with warm and cold fronts. They bring mainly wet and windy weather. The weather pattern associated with a frontal depression is shown in Figure 5.

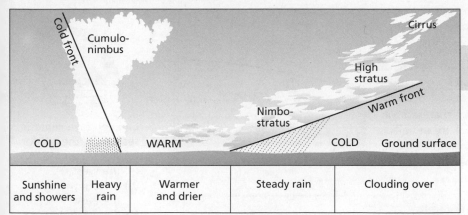

◀ *Figure 5 Cross section of a frontal depression*

Sunshine and showers	Heavy rain	Warmer and drier	Steady rain	Clouding over

The cloud and rain are caused by the warm air being forced to rise above the cold air along the fronts. The rising air cools and its moisture condenses into clouds. At the cold front the air is being forced up most strongly which is why the clouds are taller (cumulo-nimbus) and the rain is heavier (sometimes thunderstorms).

Anticyclones are areas of high pressure. They give mainly dry weather because air is sinking and warming up, making rain less likely. There is little wind.

There are differences in anticyclonic weather in the UK between summer and winter.

	Summer	**Winter**
Temperature	Higher than average Heatwaves possible	Lower than average Big freeze possible
Precipitation	Dew and mist at night	Frost and fog at night

Reasons for these differences are a combination of:
- how high an angle the sun is in the sky;
- the relative lengths of day and night.

In summer, the high angle of the sun in the sky gives high rates of insolation and daylight is more than 12 hours so that the Earth's surface is well heated up. The surface cools down at night, as heat escapes through the cloudless skies, which leads to condensation of moisture where the air is in contact with the cold ground. Dew forms instead of frost because summer temperatures stay above 0°C and mist forms rather than fog because nights are short.

This is what a frontal depression looks like.

It is part of a synoptic chart (weather map).

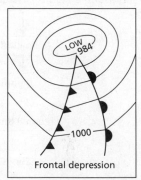

Frontal depression

This is what an anticyclone looks like.

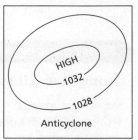

Anticyclone

Re-write the paragraph for anticyclonic weather in winter.

Begin 'In winter, the low angle of the sun in the sky ...'

List the differences between depressions and anticyclones.

Key Idea 2: weather and climate influence human activities

What you need to study and to know:

People take weather and climate into account when deciding what to do. Some of the effects upon peoples' activities in the UK are shown in Figure 1.

Sometimes the weather is more severe or different from what is usually expected. The effects on people are greater because they less likely to have been planned for. However, people in MEDCs are usually able to cope better than those in LEDCs. Two types of severe weather that affect many people are:
- drought;
- tropical storms and high winds.

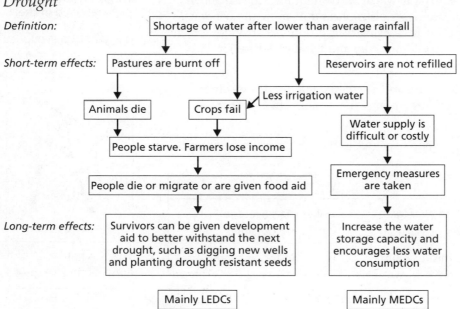

Water storage
Dairy farming

Crop growing

Crop growing (cereals and root crops)
Seaside holiday resorts

Dairy farming
Flowers and early vegetables
Seaside holiday resorts

◀ *Figure 1 Human activities in different parts of the UK*

Can you give climatic reasons in the UK for:
(a) water storage in the west
(b) crop growing in the east
(c) dairy farming in the west
(d) seaside resorts in the south?

Drought

Definition: Shortage of water after lower than average rainfall

Short-term effects: Pastures are burnt off   Reservoirs are not refilled

Animals die   Crops fail   Less irrigation water

Water supply is difficult or costly

People starve. Farmers lose income

People die or migrate or are given food aid

Emergency measures are taken

Long-term effects: Survivors can be given development aid to better withstand the next drought, such as digging new wells and planting drought resistant seeds

Increase the water storage capacity and encourages less water consumption

Mainly LEDCs   Mainly MEDCs

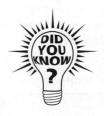

There are always some people who benefit from disasters.

In the UK's 'drought' of 1995, the following people did well financially:
- makers of soft drinks;
- breweries;
- ice cream makers and sellers;
- seaside hotel owners.

Fog is another weather hazard. List how it causes problems for:
- road traffic;
- aeroplanes;
- shipping.

Know your case study

Drought in Ethiopia in 1983-4

Short term effects:
- about 500 000 people died, especially the young and the elderly;
- many more needed relief aid, mainly food aid, organized by charities in MEDCs;
- people migrated from areas that were too remote to receive food aid, many ending up in refugee camps in the Sudan.

Long term effects:
- about 500 000 people, who are malnourished and poverty stricken, still need some food aid;
- more aid is now in the form of development aid to increase agricultural output to give people more security for the future.

Tropical storms and high winds

These are very intense areas of low pressure which have different names in different parts of the world. For example, they are called hurricanes in the Caribbean and cyclones in Bangladesh. They can cause great damage because of:

- high winds up to 300km per hour;
- heavy rain up 500mm in 24 hours;
- storm surges with waves up to 10m high.

The short-term effects of tropical storms can be total destruction. The wind is strong enough to flatten everything in its way – homes, shops, power lines, trees and crops. Landslides and mud flows are set off on slopes by the heavy rain and these wash away homes, roads and bridges. Low-lying and coastal areas are flooded, destroying settlements and farm land. Following hurricane warnings in September 1998, more than one million people were evacuated from New Orleans before Hurricane Georges arrived. Otherwise there would have been great loss of life, as happened in the Dominican Republic.

The long term effects are less in MEDCs where governments and insurance companies are more likely to pay for homes to be re-built. In LEDCs, survivors of the storm, who are already poor, have to start again. It may take several years for homes, roads and bridges to be re-built and for bush and tree crops to start producing again.

Test Yourself

Make notes for a case study: Hurricane Georges, September 1998

Use Figure 2 as well.

Mention:
- number dead and missing;
- types of damage caused;
- estimated cost of the damage;
- differences between what happened in the USA and elsewhere.

Examination practice question

(a) (i) State two characteristics of a frontal depression.   (2 marks)

   (ii) Explain why there are usually periods of rain when a frontal depression passes over the UK.   (5 marks)

(b) Study Figure 2.

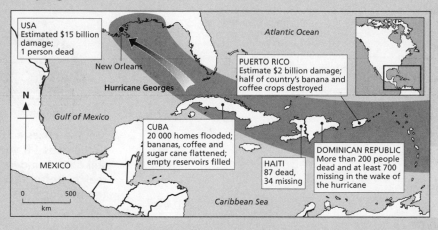

Figure 2 Short term effects of Hurricane Georges in September 1998

   (i) Give evidence from Figure 2 which shows that more than 1000 people could have died.   (1 mark)

   (ii) Name the one benefit of the hurricane mentioned in Figure 2.   (1 mark)

   (iii) Why is the income from exporting crops from the Caribbean countries likely to be reduced this year and for the next few years?   (2 marks)

(c) Explain why climatic hazards, such as tropical storms and drought, often cause more loss of life in LEDCs than MEDCs.   (4 marks)

[Check your answers on page 124]   Total: 15 marks

Summary

Key words from the syllabus

anticyclone	fog	temperature
climate	precipitation	tropical storm
depression	prevailing winds	weather
drought	synoptic chart	

Write down a definition for each of the key words. Check them with those given on page 44.

Checklist for revision

	Understand and know	Need more revision	Do not understand	Hints and tips
I can name the four main factors which affect the temperature of a place	☐	☐	☐	pp 78-9
I understand what is meant by insolation	☐	☐	☐	p 78
I can give reasons why the British Isles is warmer than would be expected for its latitude in winter	☐	☐	☐	p 78
I can explain why the south of the UK is warmer than the north in the summer	☐	☐	☐	p 80
I understand why the isotherms in the British Isles run from north to south in the winter	☐	☐	☐	p 80
I can give two different reasons why the west of the British Isles is wetter than the east	☐	☐	☐	p 81
I can explain why frontal rainfall occurs	☐	☐	☐	pp 82-3
I can describe how the weather pattern changes as warm and cold fronts pass over a place	☐	☐	☐	pp 82-3
I can explain why dry weather is more likely with an anticyclone than with a depression	☐	☐	☐	pp 84
I understand how drought affects people	☐	☐	☐	pp 86-7
I understand why tropical storms can cause so much damage	☐	☐	☐	p 88

Hints and Tips!

The page numbers refer to where the topic can be found in your text book *Understanding GCSE Geography.* If you don't understand the topic read the relevant section in your text book, make some notes and learn about it.

Tick the boxes and fill in the gaps – if you still do not understand seek help from your teacher.

Know your case studies

Which real places have you studied as an example of...
- a drought   name:_____ pp 86-7, 228-9
- a tropical storm   name:_____ p 88

7 Ecosystems

Key Ideas
1 Different ecosystems can be identified.
2 Human activity has an impact on natural ecosystems.

Exam Watch

A question on this topic appears in Section B in your first written paper.

It is a 15 mark question and it will be Question 10.

Key words and definitions

biodiversity	great numbers of plants and animals living in an ecosystem
coniferous woodland	forests consisting of species of conifers such as pine and spruce
ecosystem	includes the living communities of plants and animals and the physical elements upon which they depend, such as climate and soil
hydrology	water movements both on the surface and underground
slash and burn	clearing of the forest by subsistence farmers for cultivation
soil	loose material below the surface, which is a mixture of minerals, organic material, air and water
tropical rain forests	dense jungle which grows in hot, wet climates near the Equator

Key Idea 1: different ecosystems can be identified
What you need to study and to know:

A *The world distribution of ecosystems, especially coniferous woodlands and tropical rain forests, and the reasons for it*

B *The characteristics of the vegetation and nature of the soils*
   (i) in coniferous woodlands
   (ii) in tropical rain forests
   and the reasons for them.

Definition of an ecosystem
This is a living community of plants and animals and the physical factors upon which they depend, such as climate and soil. These four elements are shown in Figure 1.

Climate goes at the top because, on a world scale, this is the most important factor. It determines the nature and extent of the vegetation cover and its soil type.

The arrows show that some of the relationships are two way. For example, vegetation is strongly affected by climate because plants can't grow without heat and water. However, vegetation also affects the climate. Leaves release water into the atmosphere by transpiration which provides moisture for more rain. There is evidence in some tropical areas, where the vegetation has been cleared, that the rainfall is lower than it used to be.

Test Yourself

Cover up the definitions of the key words and see how many you know.

Test Yourself

Cover up Figure 1. Practise drawing the diagram so that you can draw it quickly in an exam.

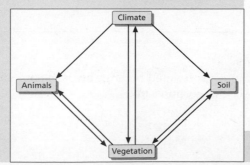

◀ *Figure 1 An ecosystem*

A The world distribution of ecosystems and the reasons for it

Although all plants need heat and water for growth, they are not needed in the same amounts. Vegetation in tropical rain forests needs plenty of both heat and water. This is why these forests are distributed around the Equator.

Summary of the Equatorial climate:
- hot all year (average 27°C)
- wet all year
- high total annual rainfall (about 2000mm).

There are so many species of trees in tropical rain forests that the names of only a few, such as mahogany and teak, are well known.

The variety of trees and plants is greater in the rain forests than anywhere else on Earth. This great variety is called **biodiversity**.

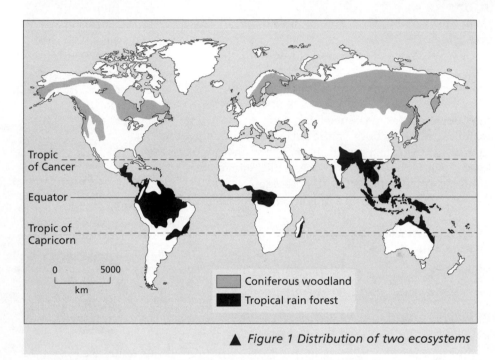

▲ *Figure 1 Distribution of two ecosystems*

Hints and Tips!

A possible exam question based on Figure 1 could be: 'Describe the distribution of rain forests.'

- state where they are found in relation to latitude;
- name the continents where they are located;
- state where the largest areas are found;
- name some of the countries in which they are found.

The climate in the temperate continental interiors, mainly between 50° and 60° north of the Equator, where coniferous trees grow, is very different.

Summary of the temperate continental climate:
- very cold winters (well below 0°C) with strong cold winds;
- short warm summers (around 17°C);
- low annual precipitation (usually under 500mm).

Only a few types of tree, such as pine and spruce, can survive the cold winter temperatures and grow in the short summer. There is no biodiversity here; stretching for hundreds of kilometres, the forests look the same.

Cover the page.

Check that you know the climate figures for
(a) Equatorial
(b) temperate continental.

You will need them to explain vegetation and soils.

Activity

On Figure 1, label three countries covered by large areas of coniferous woodlands and rain forests. Suggestions are:
- Canada
- Sweden
- Russia
- Brazil
- Congo
- Malaysia.

3 (i) The characteristics of the vegetation and nature of the soils in coniferous woodlands and the reasons for them

Characteristics of:		
Coniferous woodlands	Coniferous trees	Podsol soils
Evergreen	Conical shape	Decaying pine needles and cones on the surface
One layer of trees	Downward sloping branches	Dark, narrow layer of humus
Only one or two types of tree	Needle leaves	Grey layer forming the A horizon
Dark with the trees growing close together	Thick bark	Reddish-brown layer forming the top of the B horizon
Thick mat of dead needles on forest floor	Shallow roots	Orange-yellow layer forming the rest of the B horizon

◄ *Figure 2 Coniferous woodlands, trees and podsol soils*

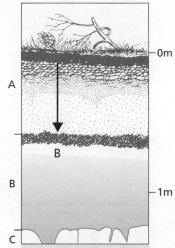

▲ Figure 3 Podsol soil. For an explanation of the letters for the soil horizons, see Figure 3 on page 54.

It is possible to identify five characteristics of coniferous trees and woodlands to show how they are adapted to the climate.

Characteristic	Adaptation
Conical shape	they are flexible and bend in strong winds
Downward sloping branches	snow slides off them more quickly
Needle leaves	water loss by transpiration is reduced because water is not plentiful (ground frozen in winter and low annual precipitation)
Thick bark	protects tree from the great winter cold
Evergreen	summers are short and growth must begin as quickly as possible when it is warm enough

The main effect of climate on the formation of the podsol soil is that precipitation is greater than evapo-transpiration. This means that:
- water drains downwards through the soil;
- the water carries organic materials and minerals;
- iron and clay are leached (washed out) of the A horizon leaving it a grey colour;
- irons and clays are re-deposited at the top of the B horizon making it reddish-brown.

Vegetation also affects soil formation. Needles from the conifers decay slowly. They add little humus to trap the minerals and stop them from being washed downwards.

Test Yourself

Describe the distribution of coniferous woodlands shown in Figure 1. Use the hints and tips on the opposite page as a guide.

DID YOU KNOW

The movement of minerals downwards through the soil is called leaching.

B (ii) The characteristics of the vegetation and nature of the soils in tropical rain forests and the reasons for them

The plants here love the great heat and humidity. The only thing that restricts their growth is the fierce competition with other plants to grab a share of the sunlight. Five layers can be seen in tropical forests (Figure 1) compared with just one in coniferous woodlands.

A Discontinuous canopy of tree crowns of the tallest trees (called emergents)

B Continuous layer of the main canopy formed by the crowns of the many tall trees

C Discontinuous under-canopy of trees between 10m and 20m high

D Layer of shrubs and young trees

E Herb layer with ferns 6m or more high

Without looking back to earlier pages, can you also remember
(a) the world distribution of tropical rain forests?
(b) the data for the Equatorial climate?

◄ *Figure 1 Characteristics of tropical rain forest vegetation.*

◄ *Figure 2 Latosol soils*

The characteristics of the tallest trees are:
- 40 – 50 metres high;
- branches only in the crowns at the top;
- leaves with extended points called drip tips;
- thin barks;
- shallow roots which extend above ground as buttresses.

Many of these forest and tree characteristics only exist because of the all year high temperatures and high rainfall. They include:
- the great density of vegetation (often referred to as jungle);
- the great variety of plants (known as biodiversity);
- the great height of the tallest trees (example mahogany);
- the forests are evergreen (plants can grow all year);
- the trees have thin barks (no need for protection against cold).

Climate is the main factor for all of these.

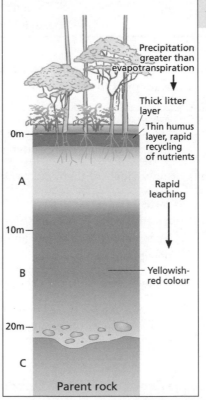

Precipitation greater than evapotranspiration

Thick litter layer

Thin humus layer, rapid recycling of nutrients

Rapid leaching

Yellowish-red colour

Parent rock

Cover up Figure 1. Draw your own sketch of a rain forest. Label the features of the forests and trees.

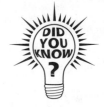

A typical soil profile has four horizons. Each one is given a letter; see Figure 3.

The soils which form under tropical rain forests are called latosols. They are a red or yellowish-red colour and are much deeper than the podsol. However, their formation is similar because they are also formed by leaching; organic materials and minerals are washed downwards because rainfall is greater than evapo-transpiration. We can say, therefore, that the high rainfall of the Equatorial climate is the main factor for latosols formation.

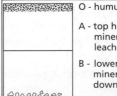
O - humus layer
A - top horizon (from which minerals may have been leached out)
B - lower horizon (into which minerals are washed down)
C - layer of weathered rock

▲ *Figure 3*

Key Idea 2: human activity has an impact on natural ecosystems
What you need to study and to know:

Large areas of tropical rain forest have survived longer than any other type of forest. They were areas of low population density. People did not find them attractive for settlement because:
- the amount and density of vegetation made access difficult, except along rivers and coasts;
- it is hot and humid for working and there are many insect pests;
- farmers who cleared the forests found that the latosol soils were less fertile than they had expected.

Wouldn't you have thought that soils which could support such a great mass of vegetation would be fertile? Figure 4 shows what happens to the soils when the trees are removed. There are no trees to supply new nutrients. Instead the nutrients already in the soil are washed out of it by the heavy rain and increased surface runoff. In the worst cases, soil erosion leaves a bare surface – red desert replaces green jungle.

▶ Figure 4 Before and after forest clearance

BEFORE CLEARANCE

Much rain intercepted

A   B   C

Only a small leakage of nutrients into the soil

AFTER CLEARANCE

All rain reaches the surface

No new nutrients from trees and plants

Surface run-off

Soil erosion

Large leakage into the ground

A   Decay of organic matter
B   Nutrients released
C   Nutrients taken up by plants

Know your case study

The Amazon Basin in Brazil
Why did the government encourage development in the Amazon Basin? The reasons can be split up into:
(a) economic – to make money by exporting minerals and using them in factories
– there are large amounts of iron ore, bauxite, gold and copper
(b) social   – to reduce population pressure along the east coast
– to give landless peasants the opportunity to own land
(c) political   – to gain international prestige from big road building and HEP projects.

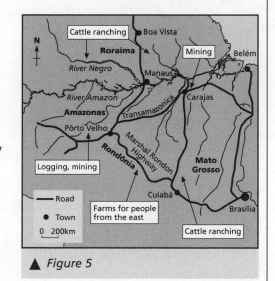

▲ Figure 5

What has been done?
Look at Figure 5 which shows that the Amazon has been opened up to farmers, loggers and miners.

What conflicts have been created?

Groups of people against forest removal	Groups of people in favour of forest removal
Hunters and collectors	Logging companies
Shifting cultivators → AMAZON ←	Miners
Rubber tappers RAIN FOREST	Cattle ranchers
Collectors of forest products	Farmers from the east

The human impact on the rain forests doesn't have to be destructive.
- Some native groups of people have successfully lived in the forests for thousands of years. By hunting, collecting and gathering, they have made use of what the forest provides for their food, medicines and tools. Their way of life totally depends upon the continued existence of the rain forests.
- Some groups from outside, such as rubber tappers, exploit natural forest products. Provided that they don't try to over-exploit the rubber by tapping the trees too frequently, the forests will remain much as they are.

These are two examples of sustainable use of rain forests.

Sometimes it makes sense for governments to conserve forests as National Parks or Wildlife Sanctuaries, particularly if this will attract tourists. In this way they make money without destroying the forest. However, many governments, like the Brazilian government, want economic development and the many natural resources in forested areas are just too attractive.

The best results come when a government is willing to plan for the future. Even logging, which means taking wood from the forests, can be a sustainable activity if properly managed. Proper management means:
- making a survey of the area's resources before using them;
- selecting only a few trees per hectare;
- cutting down only fully-grown trees;
- re-planting to replace those cut down;
- checking that the work is done according to the plans.

Sustainable use means preserving natural features so that humans can continue to benefit from them for many years into the future.

Make a list of the advantages of keeping the rain forests.

Metres

◀ *Figure 1*

Cover up the top of the page. Don't look back.

Try to answer the Exam practice question unseen.

Examination practice question

(a) Define the term ecosystem.   (3 marks)

(b) Study Figure 1 which shows a part of the tropical rain forest ecosystem.

   (i) On Figure 1, mark and label the different forest layers.   (4 marks)

   (ii) Explain why the variety of plants and density of vegetation is greatest in the tropical rain forest ecosystem.   (4 marks)

(c) Outline two ways in which people may use rain forests in a sustainable way.   (4 marks)

[Check your answers on page 124]   Total: 15 marks

Summary

Key words from the syllabus

coniferous woodland	hydrology	soil
ecosystem	slash and burn	tropical rain forests

Checklist for revision

	Understand and know	Need more revision	Do not understand	Hints and tips
I know what an ecosystem is	☐	☐	☐	p 90
I can describe some features of coniferous trees	☐	☐	☐	p 92
I know where the largest areas of coniferous woodland in the world are found	☐	☐	☐	p 90
I can give the main features of the cold continental climate where conifers are the main vegetation	☐	☐	☐	p 92
I know three ways in which coniferous trees adapt to this climate	☐	☐	☐	p 92
I can describe the colour difference between the A and B horizons in a podsol soil	☐	☐	☐	p 93
I know what is meant by leaching	☐	☐	☐	p 93
I can draw a labelled sketch to show the features of the vegetation in a tropical rain forest	☐	☐	☐	p 94
I know what the climate is like in areas with rain forests	☐	☐	☐	p 95
I can give some of the features of a latosol	☐	☐	☐	p 95
I can state three reasons why rain forests are being cleared	☐	☐	☐	p 96
I understand how the nutrient cycle changes once the forest has been cleared	☐	☐	☐	p 97
I understand what is meant by sustainable management of forests	☐	☐	☐	pp 98-9
I can list advantages for preserving the world's forested areas	☐	☐	☐	p 98

Test Yourself

?

Write down a definition for each of the key words. Check them with those given on page 51.

Hints and Tips!

The page numbers refer to where the topic can be found in your text book *Understanding GCSE Geography*. If you don't understand the topic read the relevant section in your text book, make some notes and learn about it.

Test Yourself

Tick the boxes and fill in the gaps – if you still do not understand seek help from your teacher.

Know your case studies

Which real places have you studied as an example of...
- an area where tropical rain forest has been cleared name:_____ pp 96-7
- sustainable methods of forest management name:_____ pp 98-9

8 Population

Key Ideas
1 The global distribution of population is uneven.
2 Population change depends upon birth rate, death rate and migration.
3 Population change presents opportunities and problems.

A 25 mark question on this topic will be Question 1 on the second geography written paper.

You either answer the question on population or the one on settlement.

Key words and definitions

annual population growth rate	the rate at which a population is increasing owing to natural increase and migration, i.e. birth rate minus death rate, plus or minus migration
census	a questionnaire every ten years to find out the population characteristics of a country
Crude Birth Rate	the number of births per 1000 population in one year
Crude Death Rate	the number of deaths per 1000 population in one year
Demographic Transition Model	a model showing the stages of growth of a country's population
density	the number of people per unit area, e.g. per square kilometre
distribution	the spread of people over an area
infant mortality rates	the number of deaths per 1000 children under one year old in a country per year
life expectancy	the average number of years a person is expected to live
migration	the movement of people
Natural Increase	the increase (or decrease) in a population found by the birth rate minus the death rate and normally expressed as a percentage
population policies	plans and laws passed by governments to help either to increase or decrease a country's population
population pyramid	a graph to show the population structure or age-sex composition of a population
population structure	the age and sex composition of a country, region or city
pull factors	factors which attract a person to a place
push factors	factors which force a person away from a place
refugee	a person forced to move from one country to another, often as a result of war or famine

Key Idea 1: the global distribution of population is uneven
What you need to study and to know:
- the world pattern of population is uneven – some parts of the world are very densely populated while others are almost empty of people;
- where people live is explained by physical and human factors;
- high population densities are usually found in areas with a favourable climate, where food can be easily grown and where there are good communications and resources;
- low population densities are usually found in areas with harsh climates, poor soils, mountainous relief and where communications are poor.

Hints and Tips!
It is essential that you understand the acronyms MEDC and LEDC for this unit of work.

MEDC = More **E**conomically **D**eveloped **C**ountry

LEDC = Less **E**conomically **D**eveloped **C**ountry

The world distribution of population

The world distribution of population is uneven. Some parts of the world are densely populated, having many people, while others are sparsely populated with very few people.

Explaining the population distribution

Figure 1 shows some of the physical factors (relief and climate) which limit population density. Other physical factors include soils, vegetation, accessibility and resources. Figure 2 shows how human factors such as communications, labour, political policies and cultural factors may also affect population densities.

What is meant by the terms *sparsely populated* and *densely populated*?

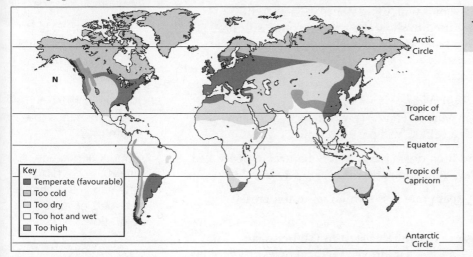

Key
- ■ Temperate (favourable)
- □ Too cold
- □ Too dry
- □ Too hot and wet
- ■ Too high

Arctic Circle
Tropic of Cancer
Equator
Tropic of Capricorn
Antarctic Circle

◄ *Figure 1 Limitations on population density*

DID YOU KNOW?

Population density is the number of people who live in an area, measured in people per square kilometre.

► *Figure 2 Human factors affecting population density*

	High population density	Low population density
Economic	Large rich markets for trade Good communications Access to imports and exports Skilled and abundant labour	Poor trading links, small markets Poor communications Limited access Limited job opportunities
Social	Prefer to live together	Prefer to be more isolated
Political	Stable governments	Unstable governments

Know your case study

Brazil

The Amazon rainforest	The south east coast
Sparsely populated – under one person per km²	High densities – over 50 per km² but over 1000 per km² in the cities

Reasons:
- hot (28°C) and wet (2000mm) climate
- diseases spread easily, e.g. yellow fever
- thick jungle makes access difficult
- infertile soils
- remote interior location
- little employment

Reasons:
- climate less extreme
- coastal location gives good trading position
- large cities, e.g. Rio, São Paulo, with industries and commerce
- fertile soils for agriculture
- long history of settlement
- excellent communication links

Hints and Tips!

A common error is to misread questions and not to pay enough attention to the wording. Make sure you understand what are physical factors and what are human factors, and give the right information when answering a question.

Population change

Key Idea 2: population change depends upon birth rate, death rate and migration

What you need to study and to know about population change:

- world population grew only slowly until the twentieth century, then it grew very rapidly because birth rates were higher than death rates, especially in the LEDCs;
- the Demographic Transition Model describes the typical changes in a country's population over time. Most MEDCs are at stage 4 while many LEDCs are still in stages 2 or 3 with rapid population growth;
- population pyramids are used to show the age-sex composition of a population. Many LEDCs have a triangular shaped pyramid while MEDCs are more rectangular.

Crude Birth Rate is the number of live births per 1000 population per year.

Crude Death Rate is the number of deaths per 1000 population per year.

Natural increase is the birth rate minus the death rate.

Annual population growth is the birth rate minus the death rate plus or minus migration.

The Demographic Transition Model

The Demographic Transition Model (Figure 1) was designed to show the stages of population growth a MEDC will pass through.

Stage 1 High birth rates and high death rates, so low natural increase and little population growth. Very few populations in stage 1 today.

Stage 2 High birth rate but death rate falls so high natural increase and rapid population growth.

Birth rates are high because:
- no birth control
- high infant death rates
- more children to work on farms
- religious beliefs

Death rates start to fall because:
- improved medical care
- more vaccinations, hospitals, doctors
- cleaner water supplies and improved sewage facilities
- improved food supplies

Stage 3 Lower death rates and the birth rate starts to fall. The population growth rate begins to fall. LEDCs are in, or moving towards, Stage 3.

The birth rate starts to fall because of family planning, improved medical care and women marrying later.

Stage 4 Low birth and death rates. A low natural increase and steady population. Most MEDCs are at stage 4.

Complete the boxes below Figure 1.

In the birth and death rate boxes write: 'High', 'Low' or 'Decreasing'.

In the population change box write: 'Steady decrease, 'Slow increase', 'Rapid increase' or 'Steady population'.

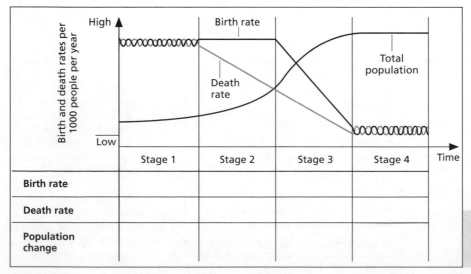

◀ Figure 1 The Demographic Transition Model

Population pyramids

A census is carried out every ten years to collect data about a country's population. The data on the ages and sex of a population can be used to draw a population pyramid. Figure 3 shows population pyramids for Ethiopia, an LEDC and France, a MEDC.

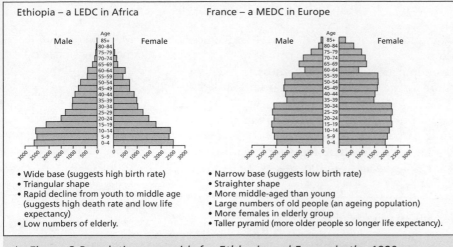

Ethiopia – a LEDC in Africa

France – a MEDC in Europe

- Wide base (suggests high birth rate)
- Triangular shape
- Rapid decline from youth to middle age (suggests high death rate and low life expectancy)
- Low numbers of elderly.

- Narrow base (suggests low birth rate)
- Straighter shape
- More middle-aged than young
- Large numbers of old people (an ageing population)
- More females in elderly group
- Taller pyramid (more older people so longer life expectancy).

▲ *Figure 2 Population pyramids for Ethiopia and France in the 1990s*

A population pyramid can be used to suggest in which stage of the Demographic Transition Model a country is in. Notice the triangular shape of Ethiopia's pyramid. The wide base and tapering sides suggest high birth and death rates typical of stage 2 in the model. France's pyramid is taller and straighter suggesting low birth and death rates. This places France in stage 4 of the model.

Some population pyramids have gaps or bulges in particular age groups. The gaps in France's pyramid are a result of the two world wars. A city in a LEDC often has a bulge in the male population between 20 and 40. This reflects the in-migration of young males from the countryside to the city in search of work.

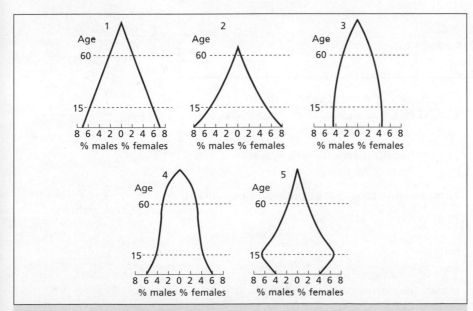

▲ *Figure 3 Population pyramids*

A population pyramid is also known as an age-sex pyramid

Test Yourself

Study Figure 3 and answer the questions which follow.

Which pyramid matches each of the following statements? Put the correct number in the box:

☐ A country with low birth rates and low death rates.

☐ A country which has had a rapid decline in its birth rate.

☐ A country where death rates have begun to fall although birth rates are still high.

☐ A country with high birth rates and high death rates.

☐ A country with a sudden increase in birth rate having had low birth and death rates.

Which pyramid best illustrates a country:
(i) in stage 2?
(ii) in stage 4?

Migration

Key Idea 2: population change depends on birth rate, death rate and migration

What you need to study and to know about migration:

- population change within a country needs to include migration as well as birth rate and death rate;
- there are different types of migration, for example, refugee movements and rural to urban migration;
- migration has many causes, some are voluntary, e.g. moving to a new house or job, while others are forced, e.g. the refugees from Kosova in 1999;
- migrations are a result of both pull factors, e.g. new job, warmer climate, and push factors, e.g. famine, lack of services;
- migrations have both advantages and disadvantages for the migrants as well as for the countries they leave and resettle in.

Types of migration

Figure 1 shows there are many different types of migration.

	International (across national borders)	Internal (within a country)
Voluntary (people choose to move)	Rich to rich, e.g. UK doctors to USA; Poor to rich, e.g. Mexicans to California.	Urban to rural, e.g. from London to Cornwall for retirement; Urban to urban, e.g. from Derby to Sheffield for a new job; Rural to urban, e.g. from the Scottish Highlands to Glasgow.
Forced (no choice)	From drought-hit countries, e.g. Ethiopia; Refugees from Kosova due to Serb ethnic cleansing; Palestinians to Jordan; Monserratians to escape the volcanic eruptions.	The Bosnians in Yugoslavia; Russians to Siberia.

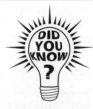

The causes of migration

Forced migration may have either physical or human causes:

Physical: earthquakes, floods, volcanic activity, drought, famine.

Human: war, religious or political persecution.

People have no choice about moving and many are forced to cross international boundaries as refugees.

Voluntary migration is when the migrant makes the decision to move, based upon a series of pull and push factors.

Migration is the movement of people.

Emigration is the movement out of a country.

Immigration is the movement into a country.

The migration balance is the difference between emigration and immigration.

◀ *Figure 1 Types of migration*

Hints and Tips!

Take care with a question on push and pull factors in an exam. Don't fall into the trap of writing:

'The pull factors are more jobs and better services; the push factors are no jobs and poor services.'

Jobs and services will only be marked once. Try to include a wider range of different factors. Also, make sure your factors are specific: 'Jobs' may be true, but it is vague. 'Jobs, e.g. with the car firms VW and Fiat in São Paulo' is better. 'Formal sector jobs with the car firms VW and Fiat in São Paulo' is better still!

Push factors are the disadvantages of where people live, forcing them away from the area.

Pull factors are the attractions or advantages of where people are moving to.

The advantages and disadvantages of migration

Migrations have both advantages and disadvantages for the countries and people involved.

Know your case study

International migration – the Palestinian refugees

In 1948 the Jews declared the existence of the state of Israel which replaced the country of Palestine. War broke out and many Palestinians fled as refugees to neighbouring countries such as the Lebanon. Figure 2 shows the impact of the refugee movement.

	Advantages	Disadvantages
To the Lebanon (host country)	Potential labour force	Overcrowded refugee camps; Already a poor country; Struggling to provide food, shelter and medical care; Wars with the PLO and between religious groups
To Israel (losing country)	More land for the Jews; More jobs available; Greater social unity; Easier to provide schools and synagogues with a single religion	Wars with the Lebanon; Hostility with Arab neighbours; Border attacks
To the Palestinian refugee	Free from hostility in Israel	Lost their homeland; Appalling living conditions; Little food, money, clothing; Lost their rights

Hints and Tips!

Sometimes an exam question will ask for the **impact** of a migration. There can be both positive impacts or advantages and negative impacts or disadvantages.

Remember to include both advantages and disadvantages if the question asks for the **impact** of something.

◀ *Figure 2 The impact of the Palestinian refugee crisis*

Internal migration: rural to urban migration in the developing world

	Advantages	Disadvantages
To the host city	Large labour supply; Market for goods	Creates large shanties; Shortage of housing, food, services, jobs; Pollution and congestion
To the losing rural area	Fewer mouths to feed; May receive money	Shortage of labour; Farmland abandoned; Females and old people left behind
To the migrant	More hope of a job; Earns money; Access to better services; Conditions still better than in the rural areas	Live in squalid shanties or sleep on the streets; Leave family behind

Cover this page and write down the impact of:
(a) the Palestinian refugee crisis in the Lebanon
(b) rural to urban migration in an LEDC.

Did you remember to include both advantages and disadvantages?

◀ *Figure 3 The impact of rural to urban migration in LEDCs*

The impact of population change

Key Idea 3: population change creates opportunities but may also cause problems

What you need to study and to know:
- population growth has advantages, e.g. provides a large workforce, and disadvantages, e.g. the environmental impact;
- many LEDCs are concerned about high population growth and have policies to try to reduce growth, e.g. birth control;
- LEDCs also implement irrigation schemes and exploit their resources in order to cope with the needs of a rising population;
- some MEDCs have reclaimed and drained land in order to accommodate larger populations;
- many MEDCs are concerned about ageing populations and falling birth rates.

The world population is growing but this hides great differences around the world. In some MEDCs the population is steady or even falling while in the LEDCs the population growth is still high. Figure 1 shows that an increase or a decrease in population have both advantages and disadvantages.

	Advantages	Disadvantages
Steady or declining population (mostly MEDCs)	Less demand on services; Less pollution of air, land and water	Smaller workforce; Weaker economy; Loss of status; Ageing population
High population growth (LEDCs)	Large workforce and potential market for goods	Provision of housing, jobs, services can't keep pace; Congestion, overcrowding; Vast shanty towns and the loss of farmland to city sprawl; Pollution of air, land and water; Poverty; Overgrazing and overcultivation; Soil erosion and desertification; Deforestation

Look through all the disadvantages on Figure 1. Put an E beside all of those which have an impact on the environment.

◀ *Figure 1*

Solving population problems in LEDCs

LEDCs have two main problems to cope with:
(i) high population growth caused by high birth rates;
(ii) the consequences of high population growth.

Controlling population growth

Most LEDCs attempt to control their birth rate. This is achieved in a variety of ways:
- family planning policies and contraceptive advice, e.g. China;
- encouraging women to become better educated and to have careers;
- improving health care so fewer children die;
- encouraging later marriages.

Cover up the page.

What are the two main problems the LEDCs must try to solve?

Coping with the consequences of high population growth

In LEDCs the high population growth means:
- environmental problems, e.g. pollution, soil erosion;
- socio-economic problems, e.g. unemployment and poverty;
- political problems, e.g. how to stop sprawling cities and provide enough space, food, housing and services for the whole population.

The governments of some LEDCs, such as Brazil and Indonesia, have chosen to clear more land in order to provide more space for their growing population. In others, such as Egypt, land has been reclaimed and irrigated in order to increase the food supply and to provide more living space. In China, the government has chosen to introduce birth control.

Resource exploitation means the use of natural resources such as land, minerals and vegetation to provide for the population.

Irrigation is the artificial watering of the land

Know your case study

Indonesia and China

Indonesia – transmigration

Java, the main island of Indonesia, has 60 per cent of the population and is very overcrowded. The population continues to grow as more and more people move to the island and especially to Jakarta, the capital city, looking for work. The government has tried to solve the problem by resource exploitation and transmigration. This involves clearing areas of the rain forest on some of the other islands of Indonesia and setting up farmland with houses. People from Java volunteer to be transmigrated or moved to these new settlements. They are given free transport and help with food and fertilizer. The scheme is very popular but it has not reduced the overcrowding problem in Java. There have been other problems too:
- costs are very high;
- some of the soils are infertile and 10 per cent of settlements fail;
- destruction of the rain forest and loss of wildlife;
- conflict between the locals and the migrants.

The one-child policy in China

China introduced the one-child policy to try to achieve a stable population of about 1.2 billion early in the twenty-first century. The policy is very strict. Incentives are used such as free education, housing and pension benefits for those who stick to one child. There are age limits for when people can marry, and permission is needed to marry and to have a child. There are also reports of fines, forced abortions and sterilizations for those who try to have more than one child. The policy has worked well in the cities but in the countryside large families are still wanted to work in the fields. There have also been reports of genocide. The girl babies are being killed because boys are held in greater esteem. In the future China may be a nation with many spoilt children who will grow up to struggle to find partners because of the shortage of women.

Cover this page and see what you can remember about the case studies.

(a) What is resource exploitation and irrigation?

(b) For both case studies in Indonesia and China:
- state the aim of the scheme
- describe the scheme
- list its advantages and disadvantages.

Hints and Tips!

Check through your answers – how many real details or place names have you included. Does it really sound like Indonesia or China or could it apply to any example of resource exploitation or birth control?

Population problems in MEDCs

Too many people
Many MEDCs also needed to cope with growing populations although the rate of growth has never been as great as in LEDCs. Some MEDCs, for example, the Netherlands, created more space for housing and farmland. This was achieved by reclaiming and draining new land from the sea.

Ageing populations
Life expectancy has increased with better healthcare so there are more people living longer. Governments need to provide pensions, care homes and special health care. Perhaps some schools will close with the money being used to support the elderly. State pensions may become means tested and people will need to have private pension schemes.

Falling populations
Countries or places concerned about falling populations can use various techniques to try to increase their population:
- encourage guestworkers as in Germany after World War II
- encourage higher birth rates with high family allowances, crèches for working mothers and tax incentives
- discourage or ban the use of contraceptives.

However, such schemes are rare today because of global concerns about population growth, economic recession and unemployment and the high costs of welfare payments.

Hints and Tips!
The human geography questions have 25 marks. This means that some questions, particularly those asking for case study information, may have up to 8 or 9 marks. You need to revise and learn your work thoroughly so you can write detailed answers to these questions.

Examination practice question

(a) Study Figure 1 showing the population density in Britain in 1994.

   (i)   What is meant by the term 'population density'? (1 mark)
   (ii) Describe the distribution of areas with a low population density in Britain. (2 marks)
   (iii) Name a country or area you have studied with a high population density and explain the reasons for the high density. (6 marks)

(b) Study Figure 2.

   (i)   What is the correct name for the type of diagrams in Figure 2? (1 mark)
   (ii) Describe three differences in the shape of the diagrams for Ethiopia and France. (3 marks)
   (iii) What do the diagrams suggest about the level of development of each country? (4 marks)

(c) Using one or more examples from your studies, explain how LEDCs are trying to solve the problems caused by high population growth. (8 marks)

Total 25 marks

[Check your answers on pages 124-5]

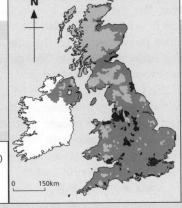

▶ Figure 1 Britain's population density in 1994

Key
Population (per km²)
■ over 150
■ 11–150
□ 0–10

0   150km

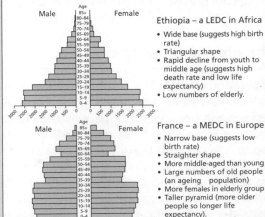

Ethiopia – a LEDC in Africa
- Wide base (suggests high birth rate)
- Triangular shape
- Rapid decline from youth to middle age (suggests high death rate and low life expectancy)
- Low numbers of elderly.

France – a MEDC in Europe
- Narrow base (suggests low birth rate)
- Straighter shape
- More middle-aged than young
- Large numbers of old people (an ageing population)
- More females in elderly group
- Taller pyramid (more older people so longer life expectancy).

▶ Figure 2 Ethiopia and France in the 1990s

Summary

Key words from the syllabus

annual population growth	birth control	census
Crude Birth rate	Crude Death Rate	Demographic Transition Model
density	distribution	drainage
emigration	fertility	immigration
infant mortality	irrigation	land reclamation
life expectancy	migration	mortality
Natural Increase	population	population policies
population pyramid	population structure	pull factors
push factors	refugee	rural depopulation
zero population growth		

Checklist for revision

	Understand and know	Need more revision	Do not understand	Hints and tips
know the world distribution of population	☐	☐	☐	p 102
know the reasons for the distribution (physical and human)	☐	☐	☐	pp 103-5
know the components of population change (NI = BR-DR +/– Migration)	☐	☐	☐	p 106
can draw and label the stages in the Demographic Transition Model (DTM)	☐	☐	☐	p 107
can draw population pyramids for stages 2 and 4 in the DTM	☐	☐	☐	pp 107-8
know the different types and causes of migration	☐	☐	☐	p 116
know the advantages and disadvantages of emigration and immigration	☐	☐	☐	pp 117-121
know that population change can have both advantages and disadvantages	☐	☐	☐	pp 109, 110, 113
know the environmental effects of population growth	☐	☐	☐	p 113

Hints and Tips!

The page numbers refer to where the topic can be found in your text book *Understanding GCSE Geography.* If you don't understand the topic read the relevant section in your text book, make some notes and learn about it.

Test Yourself

Read through the list of key words checking that you understand the meaning of, and can define, each one.

Tick the boxes and fill in the gaps – if you still do not understand seek help from your teacher.

Know your case studies

Which real places have you studied as an example of...

● high population density	name:_____	pp 104-5
● low population density	name:_____	pp 104-5
● types of migration	name:_____	pp 116-22
● policy of birth control	name:_____	p 112
● policy to increase population growth	name:_____	p 110
● environmental impact of population growth	name:_____	p 113
● irrigation	name:_____	p 115
● resource exploitation	name:_____	p 114
● land reclamation and drainage	name:_____	p 111

9 Settlement

Key Ideas
1 Settlements vary in site, size, structure and function
2 Urbanization is a global phenomenon
3 Planning strategies are needed to control urban growth

A 25 mark question on this topic will be Question 2 on the second geography written paper.

You either answer the question on settlement or the question on population.

Key words and definitions

Central Business District (CBD)	the city centre with shops, offices and entertainment facilities
function of settlement	the 'work' or purpose of a settlement, such as a tourist resort
Green Belt	an area of land around a town or city protected from development in order to halt the expansion of towns into the countryside
hierarchy of settlement	settlements arranged in order of importance
inner city	the zone of mixed land uses around the CBD developed in Victorian times
morphology	the arrangement of land use zones in an urban area
rural-urban fringe	the area beyond the suburbs where there is a mixture of rural and urban land uses
settlement	a place where people live, anything from an isolated farm to a vast sprawling urban area called a megalopolis
shanty town	a squatter settlement, often sited on the fringes of large cities in LEDCs
site	the physical land on which a settlement is built
sphere of influence	the distance people are prepared to travel to use the shops and services in a settlement, sometimes called the trade area
sprawl	the uncontrolled expansion of towns and cities into the countryside
urban zone	land uses in a town cluster together into zones giving industrial areas, housing areas, shopping areas
urbanization	a process whereby a greater proportion of people are concentrated into towns and cities

Key Idea 1: settlements vary in site, size, structure and function
What you need to study and to know:
- the availability of a water supply, aspect and shelter, defence, resources and communications affected where settlements were sited;
- settlements can be arranged into a hierarchy based upon population size, services and sphere of influence;
- settlements have different functions, e.g. tourist town, and these can change;
- towns and cities can be divided into distinct zones, e.g. the CBD, residential zones. This is urban morphology;
- the urban morphology of cities in MEDCs is different to that in LEDCs.

Hints and Tips!
It is essential that you understand the acronyms MEDC and LEDC for this unit of work.

MEDC = **M**ore **E**conomically **D**eveloped **C**ountry

LEDC = **L**ess **E**conomically **D**eveloped **C**ountry

The easiest way to throw marks away in the examination is to answer a question using MEDC examples when the question asked for LEDCs or vice versa.

Cover up the definitions. See how many you can do.

The site of a settlement

Settlements are places where people live and work. Settlement began many thousands of years ago and today there is a range of different-sized settlements from individual farms to huge sprawling cities.

The site of a settlement is the physical land on which it is built. Early settlements were sited with great care and several physical factors were very important:

- **Water supply**: a river, stream, well or spring was needed. These are wet-point sites. In some areas the land was marshy and prone to flooding so settlements sited on dry-point sites – terraces or gravel mounds away from the threat of floods.
- **Aspect and shelter**: in Britain many settlements were sited on south-facing slopes and on lower hillsides. These sites were warmer and sheltered from cold northerly winds.
- **Defence**: many settlements have the remains of walls, castles or forts. Others are built where the physical geography gives a good defensive position such as a hilltop, a gap between hills or a meander.
- **Resources**: food, fuel and building materials were essential for early settlements. Areas with fertile soils often supported many settlements and a local woodland would be used for fuel and building materials.
- **Communications**: some settlements were sited at a bridging point or at a gap through hills. These settlements became a focus for transport routes and often grew as a route focus attracting trade from other settlements. These settlements often grew because of a good situation.

Today many of these reasons for settlement location are unimportant. We no longer need to protect ourselves from attack or provide our own food, water and fuel.

DID YOU KNOW?

Situation is the location of a settlement in relation to the surrounding area. A good situation would be a route focus which encouraged trade with nearby settlements causing the settlement to grow.

Know your case study

Know your case study: Berwick-upon-Tweed, England

Figure 1 is an annotated sketch map to show the site of Berwick upon Tweed.

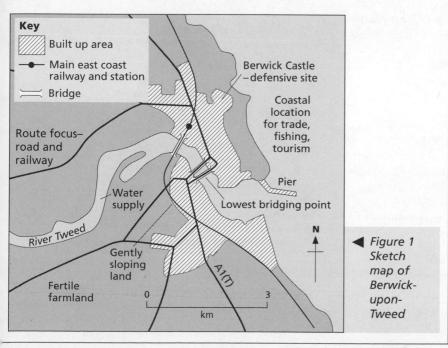

Figure 1 Sketch map of Berwick-upon-Tweed

Test Yourself

Make sure you can describe the site of a settlement you have studied and draw an annotated sketch map to show its site.

For Berwick-upon-Tweed:
- describe and explain its site
- explain why Berwick grew into a town.

The functions of a settlement

The function of a settlement is its purpose – why it is there and the 'work' it does. Functions include:

- residential – providing housing;
- industrial – includes traditional heavy and modern light industries;
- administrative – government and council offices;
- commercial – the shops and financial services;
- educational – schools, colleges and universities.

Settlements can be classified according to their function, for example, mining towns, resort towns and ports. Most large towns and cities have several functions – they are multi-functional.

Function may change over time

Many settlements have changed their functions over time, e.g. the defensive function of places like Corfe Castle and Berwick no longer applies. Study the case study below to see what changes took place in a village in County Durham.

Know your case study

Shincliffe in County Durham

In the Middle Ages Shincliffe was a small farming village. During the Industrial Revolution coal was discovered and a mine opened. Shincliffe became a mining village with a pit head, railway, colliery terraces, a school and public houses. The population grew. In the twentieth century the mine closed and people moved away looking for work in other pits. Since the 1970s Shincliffe's function has changed again. Modern housing estates have been added and most people are commuters living in Shincliffe but working in the nearby towns and cities. Shincliffe is now a commuter or dormitory village.

Test Yourself

Cover this page. Give two examples of rural settlements and two examples of urban settlements.

Write definitions for hierarchy of settlement and sphere of influence.

Explain why large settlements have a greater number and variety of shops and services.

Settlement hierarchy

A hierarchy of settlement (Figure 1) arranges the settlements in order of size or importance. The hierarchy is usually shown as a pyramid based upon:

- settlement size (population);
- the range and number of services;
- the sphere of influence.

At the top of the hierarchy in Britain are conurbations. These are very large urban areas with a large population. At the bottom of the hierarchy are isolated farms often with only one family living there. There are very few conurbations but many isolated farms – the reason why the pyramid shape of the diagram is used.

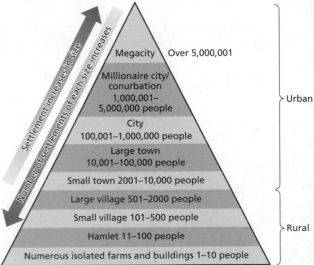

▲ Figure 1 Settlement hierarchy based on population size

Services: the larger a settlement the greater the number and variety of services to provide the local population with its needs.

Sphere of influence: the larger the settlement the greater the number and variety of shops and services and the wider the area (or sphere of influence) from which people will travel to use the centre.

Urban growth

Key Idea 2: urbanization is a global phenomenon

What you need to study and to know:

- urbanization is a process in which a higher percentage of the population lives in towns and cities;
- urbanization has occurred in every country in the world but it has been different in LEDCs and MEDCs;
- urbanization has led to the growth of urban areas and especially the growth of the very largest cities, most of which are now in the LEDCs

Urbanization in MEDCs began during the Industrial Revolution in the nineteenth century:

Agricultural revolution (machinery replaced labour)	Industrial Revolution (new factories, mines, shipyards in towns)

↓ ↓

People gradually moved from the countryside to the towns

↓

Housing was built for the workers close to the factories

↓

Towns expanded into cities and into conurbations

↓

Urbanization occurred and over 80 per cent of people in Britain now live in urban areas

Urbanization in LEDCs began much later – in the middle of the twentieth century:

Rural push factors (poor harvests, lack of money, few services)	Urban pull factors (job opportunities, education, healthcare)

↓ ↓

Rural to urban migration

↓

People flooded to the cities at a much faster rate than in the MEDCs

↓

Lower death rates and high birth rates in the cities

↓

Massive urban growth and a high rate of urbanization although still only about 30 per cent live in urban areas

World urbanization

In the twentieth century urbanization has been very rapid especially in the cities in LEDCs. The main characteristics today are:

- LEDCs now have most of the world's largest cities (Figure 2);
- LEDCs have the largest number of people living in urban areas although it is only about 30 per cent of their population;
- MEDCs still have the highest percentage of people who live in urban areas;
- the greatest growth has been in the world's largest cities creating megacities each with over ten million people.

Test Yourself

Cover this page.

Write down a definition of urbanization.

What are the main differences between urbanization in the MEDCs and the LEDCs?

Using Figure 2, write down two features of the worlds largest cities in 1995.

List two advantages and two disadvantages of urbanization in LEDCs.

Rank order 1995
(Population in millions)

Tokyo	(26.8)
São Paulo	(16.4)
New York	(16.3)
Mexico City	(15.6)
Bombay	(15.1)
Shanghai	(15.1)
Los Angeles	(12.4)
Beijing	(12.4)
Calcutta	(11.7)
Seoul	(11.6)

Source: United Nations Population Division, 1995

▲ Figure 2 The world's largest cities in 1995

The rapid urbanization in the cities of LEDCs has advantages and disadvantages:

Advantages	Disadvantages
Stimulates the economy and farming	Huge, unplanned shanty towns
Access to better services in towns	Dreadful living conditions for many
Improved incomes even if casual work	Massive congestion and pollution
Opportunities for improvement – a step on the ladder	Highlights gap between rich and poor
People may learn some skills	Loss of the best labour in the rural areas
Eases population pressure in rural areas	

Urban land-uses: the shops, industries, housing and open spaces found in cities

Land-use zones: the distinct shopping, housing and industrial areas in cities

Morphology: the internal structure of a city, the arrangement of the land-use zones

Urban morphology

Towns and cities are not a jumble of houses, industries, shops and open spaces. Particular land-uses tend to cluster together to form land use zones, e.g. the Central Business District (CBD) where shops and offices are concentrated. Urban Models (Figures 1 and 2) try to simplify reality and show the arrangement of land-use zones in a city.

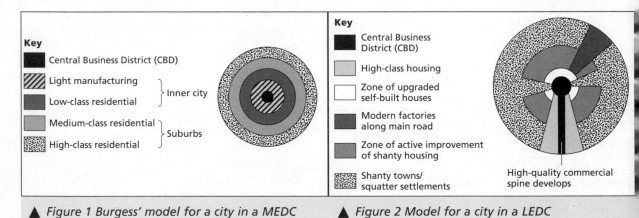

▲ Figure 1 Burgess' model for a city in a MEDC   ▲ Figure 2 Model for a city in a LEDC

Similarities and differences between cities in LEDCs and cities in MEDCs

Similarities

Both have a CBD, often in the centre of the city. The CBDs look similar with high-rise buildings and western shops. Most cities have an industrial area along a road or railway.

Differences

The MEDC city	The LEDC city
Concentric rings or sectors and rings	Less regular zones, land uses mixed
Areas for low, middle and high class housing	No middle-class zone
	Very small high-class area
Ghettos/slums in inner cities	Vast shanty towns on the edges
Traditional industries in the inner city and modern industries on estates at edge	No traditional industries
	Modern industries in zones along roads and railways

Cover this page. Practice drawing and labelling the land use models.

Urban zones

In MEDC cities, e.g. in Britain

1 The CBD
- at the centre of the city
- the original settlement site
- route focus for roads and railways
- high density of buildings
- shops, offices and entertainment facilities
- high-rise buildings and skyscrapers
- bus and rail stations at the edge
- small residential population
- high land costs

2 The inner city
- outside the CBD
- grew during Industrial Revolution
- a real mixture of land uses
- Victorian terraces
- older nineteenth-century industries
- corner shops, churches, schools, Victorian parks
- redevelopment, e.g. high rise flats

3 Suburbs
- residential housing areas
- density of housing decreases outwards
- inter-war and post-war housing closest to inner city
- modern, larger and more expensive housing on edge
- a mixture of housing types e.g. flats, semi-detached, detached and bungalows
- a mixture of council and private housing estates
- industrial estates with modern factories on the edges

4 The rural-urban fringe
- beyond the suburbs
- the edge of the built-up area
- an area of mixed land-uses
- some rural land-uses, e.g. farms, woodland
- some urban land-uses, e.g. golf courses, sewage farms, airports, motorways

In LEDC cities e.g. in Brazil

1 The CBD
- at the centre of the city
- route focus for roads and railways
- high density of buildings
- Western-style shops, offices and entertainment facilities
- high-rise buildings and skyscrapers
- small residential population
- high land costs

The CBD is often very like that of any city in the developed world.

2 The high-class sector
- close to the CBD or on a prime site, e.g. the beaches at Rio
- smart apartment blocks or detached houses with gardens

3 The shanty towns
- some are close to the CBD
- largest and most extensive on the outskirts of cities
- on wasteland, swamps or hillsides
- unplanned and illegal
- home-made shacks and shelters
- few basic services, e.g. water, sewage, electricity
- few proper roads or public transport

4 The industrial zone
- along a road or railway
- modern factory units

Test Yourself

Do this exercise for MEDC cities and LEDC cities.
(a) List the different urban zones in each city.
(b) For each urban zone write down at least two characteristic features.
(c) Write down two similarities and two differences between cities in LEDCs and cities in MEDCs.

Problems in cities of MEDCs and LEDCs

Key Idea 2: urbanization is a global phenomenon
What you need to study and to know:
- urbanization has led to urban growth which has caused problems in cities;
- in MEDCs the inner cities have declined and there are problems of congestion and decay in the CBD;
- in LEDCs urban growth has caused socio-economic and environmental problems in the CBD and in the vast shanty towns.

Problems in the CBD and inner city of MEDCs
The main problems in the CBD of developed world cities are:
- Traffic congestion – the massive growth in car ownership and commuting causes traffic jams and the need for more car parks.
- Lack of space and the high cost of land – there is a shortage of space and competition for land in the CBD so land costs are high.
- Pollution – high concentrations of traffic and people cause water, land, air and noise pollution in the CBD.
- Urban decline – parts of some CBDs have become unfashionable and have declined. Shops are boarded up, empty buildings are vandalized and covered in graffiti.

Hints and Tips!

In an exam answer never just write 'pollution' on its own. Always qualify it by saying what type of pollution and how it is caused.

The main problems in the inner cities of developed world cities are:

Environmental	Social	Economic
Decayed terraces;	Large numbers of pensioners,	Poverty and low incomes;
Poorly-built tower blocks;	students, ethnic minorities and	High unemployment;
Air and land pollution;	lone parents;	Declining industries;
Derelict buildings	High levels of disease;	High land values;
Graffiti and vandalism;	Overcrowding;	Low rates paid to local council
Traffic congestion;	High crime rates;	who have little to spend on
Lack of open space	Poor community spirit	improvements

Problems in the CBD and shanty towns of cities in LEDCs
The main problems in the CBD are very similar to those in developed world cities, but more acute. The main problems in the shanty towns in developing world cities are:

- **Housing**   illegal and unplanned;
overcrowding in the one or two roomed shacks;
shacks made of wood, corrugated iron, cardboard etc. and built so close together that they are a fire hazard;
lack of basic services, e.g. water, electricity, sewage;
no rubbish collection so litter lies in the streets.
- **Poor health**   diarrhoea, cholera and typhoid from dirty water;
health care too expensive;
little money for food so malnutrition.
- **Education**   most only ever go to primary school;
they leave early to find work to support the family.
- **Social problems**   stress, crime and vandalism
family breakdown caused by the unemployment and poverty.

Cover this page. Write down some of the problems of :
- CBDs and inner cities in MEDCs.
- CBDs and the shanty towns in LEDCs.

Make sure you can give actual examples and case study information for each one.

Attempted solutions to the problems of cities

Key Idea 3: planning strategies are needed to control urban growth

What you need to know and learn:
- in LEDCs solving the problems in the CBDs and shanty towns includes new transport systems, self-help housing schemes and new towns;
- in MEDCs problems in the CBD and inner city are being solved by traffic schemes, redevelopment and pollution control.

MRT stands for Mass Rapid Transit – these are public transport schemes like the London Underground or Newcastle Metro

Attempted solutions to the problems of cities in LEDCs
Schemes inside the city
Housing: Self-help schemes: New homes have been built as part of a scheme in São Paulo in Brazil. Building materials and basic services – water, electricity and drainage – are provided.

Transport and pollution: in São Paulo and Cairo new underground train systems reduce the numbers of commuters and traffic pollution.

Attempted solutions to problems in cities in MEDCs

Problem	Solutions
Traffic congestion in the CBD and inner city	Ring roads and by-passes to divert traffic; Pedestrianization schemes; Park and ride and MRT; Multistorey car parks
Pollution of air, land and water	Clean air acts and smokeless zones; More litter bins and road sweeping; Clean fuel technology – electric vehicles
Lack of space/high land costs in the CBD	High-rise buildings; Expansion into the inner city; Out of town shopping developments
Urban decline in the CBD	Redevelopment and new indoor shopping malls

Cover up this page and write the answers to these practice examination questions.

Using examples from your studies, describe how planners are helping to solve the problems of :
(a) cities in LEDCs
(b) cities in MEDCs.

◀ *Figure 1*

Improving the inner cities
Late 1960s: Old Victorian terraces demolished- people rehoused in high rise flats in the inner city or moved to new council estates in the suburbs. Problems with the tower blocks – damp, no privacy, no gardens, noisy, lifts and central heating always breaking down.
1980s: High rise flats need improving – some demolished some refurbished.
1990s: Local communities more involved in planning. Attempts to attract people back to the inner cities including the middle classes. Areas being gentrified – improved quality of housing and environment. More effort to bring industry and business back to the inner city to provide jobs for the residents.

Key Idea 3: planning strategies are needed to control urban growth
What you need to know and learn:
- in MEDCs there are many conflicts in the rural-urban fringe – some people believe new roads, shops and businesses are needed, others want Green Belts and conservation.

The rural-urban fringe

The rural-urban fringe surrounds the suburbs at the edge of a city. It is a zone of mixed land-uses – some rural some urban.

Should more roads and motorways be built in the rural-urban fringe?
In the 1980s car ownership and road building were encouraged. Today there is pressure on the road network but also opinions have changed. Public transport and more environmentally-friendly transport are in vogue.

Where should new business parks, shopping centres and industrial estates be built?
Out of town locations have many advantages: plenty of space, cheaper land, access to motorways and airports, access to a labour force and market in the suburbs, pleasant open countryside and cleaner, less congested environments. But these new developments increase urban sprawl, use up farmland, take trade from city centres and increase pollution and congestion in the rural-urban fringe.

Can farming survive in the rural-urban fringe?
Areas not protected by Green Belts are under pressure. Many farmers are choosing to sell their land because:
- they cannot compete for land with businesses who make higher profits;
- problems of vandalism, sheep worrying and trampling of crops;
- farmland is no longer as profitable – the beef crisis, reduced subsidies, over-production and set-aside.

Farms are rarely sold as working farms but divided up into smaller plots. They may be bought by: the large-scale developer for housing, business parks or shopping centres; or the urban dweller to practice hobby farming; or keep horses. In most cases building is likely to take place; either large scale development or greenhouses, sheds, stables and caravans. All leads to urbanization of the countryside.

Green Belts are areas of green and open land on the fringes of cities in which development is restricted. The first Green Belt was established around London in the 1950s.

There are increasing pressures to release more Green Belt areas for development. Part of the M25 around London is built on Green Belt land.

Hobby farmers are people with a plot of land to keep a few sheep and hens and grow some vegetables and fruit.

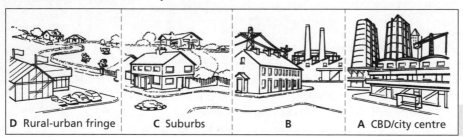

D Rural-urban fringe   C Suburbs   B   A CBD/city centre   ◀ *Figure 1*

Examination practice question

1   Study Figure 1 showing a transect of the housing in a MEDC city.

(a) (i)   What is the correct name for zone B in cities of MEDCs? (1 mark)

    (ii) Describe the characteristics of the housing in zone B. (2 marks)

    (iii) Explain the problems for people who live in zone B of a city. (6 marks)

    (iv) Describe and explain why the housing in zone C is different to that in zone B. (4 marks)

(b) (i)   Name a city in a LEDC that has attracted many new migrants causing the growth of shanty towns. (1 mark)

    (ii) Describe the main characteristics of a shanty town. (3 marks)

    (iii) Describe one or more schemes used to help solve the problems of shanty towns. (8 marks)

[Check your answers on page 125]   Total = 25 marks

Summary

Key words from the syllabus

Central Business District	settlement
function of settlement	shanty town
Green Belt	site
hierarchy of settlement	sphere of influence
inner city	sprawl
morphology	urban zone
rural-urban fringe	urbanization

Write down a definition for each of the key words. Check them with those given on page 68.

Check-list for revision

	Understand and know	Need more revision	Do not understand	Hints and tips
I know five different siting factors for settlements	☐	☐	☐	pp 124-5
I know three measures used to put settlements into a hierarchy	☐	☐	☐	p 126
I can name examples of settlements with different functions	☐	☐	☐	p 127
I can draw and describe models of urban morphology for cities in LEDCs and MEDCs	☐	☐	☐	p 130
I know the names and characteristics of the different urban zones in cities	☐	☐	☐	pp 131-8, 140-1
I know the problems of cities in LEDCs and MEDCs	☐	☐	☐	pp 133-5, 140-1
I know some ways these problems can be solved	☐	☐	☐	pp 133, 135, 142-4
In MEDCs I understand the conflicts and issues connected with the rural-urban fringe: e.g. new roads, Green Belts, urban sprawl, the need for conservation, hobby farming	☐	☐	☐	pp 138-9

Hints and Tips!

The page numbers refer to where the topic can be found in your text book *Understanding GCSE Geography*. If you don't understand the topic read the relevant section in your text book, make some notes and learn about it.

Tick the boxes and fill in the gaps – if you still do not understand seek help from your teacher.

Know your case studies

Which real places have you studied as an example of...
- the site of a settlement   name:_____ pp 124-5
- a settlement which has changed its function over time   name:_____ pp 127

The problems and solutions in:
- the CBD and inner cities in MEDCs   name:_____ pp 132-5
- shanty towns in LEDCs   name:_____ pp 140-4

10 Agriculture

Key Ideas
1 Farming as a system.
2 Agricultural activity varies from place to place.
3 Agricultural change can have advantages and disadvantages.

Exam Watch

A 25 mark question on this topic will be Question 3 on the second geography written paper.

You choose to answer either Question 3 on agriculture or Question 4 on industry.

Key words and definitions

appropriate technology	technology appropriate to the needs, skills, knowledge and wealth of the people
arable	the growing of crops, e.g. wheat, barley
capital	money
commercial	the sale of farm products for profit
extensive	a farm system using large areas of land with low inputs and outputs per hectare
farm system	a farm studied by looking at the inputs, processes and outputs
Green Revolution	the introduction of new techniques of farming and new strains of plants and animal breeds to increase yields in LEDCs
intensive	a farm system usually practised on small areas of land with high inputs and high outputs per hectare
labour	the workforce on a farm
irrigation	the artificial watering of the land by sprinklers, canals, spraying
market	the customers to buy the produce
politics	the influence of governments and trading blocs like the European Union on agriculture
soil conservation	techniques to maintain soil fertility and to reduce leaching and erosion
subsistence farming	farming in which the production is for the farmer and his family alone. No products are sold and no profits made.

Key Idea 1: farming as a system
What you need to study and to know:
- different farming types may be studied as systems with inputs, processes and outputs;
- physical factors (relief, climate and soils) and human factors (market, capital, labour and politics) result in different farming systems;
- farming systems may be commercial or subsistence, intensive or extensive;
- there is a variety of farming types in the UK, e.g. dairying in the wetter west, arable in the drier east and sheep farming in the uplands.

Test Yourself

Cover up the definitions of the key words and see how many you know already.

Activity

Which are inputs, processes or outputs? There are three of each. Well done if you can get it right!

Ploughing   Wool   Milking   Seeds   Machinery
Labour   Profit   Wheat   Harvesting

The farm as a system

Farming operates as a system with inputs, processes and outputs.

Inputs		Processes		Outputs
Physical	Human	Arable	Pastoral	
Climate	Labour	Ploughing	Milking	Crops
Soil	Seeds	Harvesting	Grazing	Animals
Relief	Animals	Weeding	Shearing	Animal products

Hints and Tips!

Be prepared to draw or complete a systems diagram for different types of farming.

Classification of farm types

Arable, pastoral, mixed	Subsistence or commercial	Intensive or extensive	Sedentary or nomadic
Arable is the growing of crops. Pastoral is the keeping of animals. Mixed is when farmers grow crops and rear animals	Subsistence farmers produce food for themselves and their family, there is no profit. Commercial farmers sell their crops and animals in order to make a profit	Intensive – high inputs of money, labour or technology to achieve high outputs or yields per hectare. The farms are usually quite small. Extensive – low inputs, large areas of land, low outputs or yields per hectare.	Sedentary is when the settlement is permanent and the landscape farmed every year. Nomadic farmers move around looking for fresh pasture or new plots to cultivate

Factors affecting farming

The type of farming in an area depends on the physical and human factors:

Human factors	Physical factors
Labour: All farms need either human labour or machinery to do the work. Some farm types use very little labour, e.g. sheep farming, others require a large labour force, e.g. rice farming in India.	Climate: Temperature – a minimum temperature of 6°C is needed for crops to grow. The growing season is the number of months the temperature is over 6°C. Different crops need a different growing season, e.g. wheat needs 90 days. Rainfall – all crops and animals need water
Market: This is the customers who buy farm produce. Farmers need to sell their crops and animals to make a profit	Relief: Temperatures decrease by 1°C every 160 metres vertical height. Uplands are more exposed to wind and rain. Steep slopes also cause thin soils and limit the use of machinery. Lowland areas are more easily farmed
Finance: Profits are used to pay the wages and to re-invest in the farm, e.g. buying seeds, fertilizer, machinery and animals	Soils: Crops grow best on deep, fertile, free-draining soils, e.g. the brown earths found in lowland Britain. Less fertile soils prone to waterlogging are best used for pastoral farming
Politics: Governments may provide subsidies and loans to encourage new farming practices but they may also place limits on production to prevent food surpluses, e.g. quotas and set-aside in the European Union	

Cover up this page.

Define these terms:
- arable, pastoral and mixed
- intensive and extensive
- commercial and subsistence
- sedentary and nomadic
- physical and human factors.

Agriculture in the European Union including the UK

Key Idea 2: agricultural activity varies from place to place

What you need to study and to know:

- at least one farm system from the UK, EU and a LEDC to include an example of commercial, subsistence, intensive and extensive systems;
- the variety of farm types in the UK include arable, hill sheep, dairying, and market gardening;
- all farm types are affected by physical and human factors;
- hill sheep farming in the UK is a commercial and extensive type of pastoral farming;
- market gardening and bulb growing in the Netherlands is a case study of a farm type in an EU country. It is commercial and intensive;
- subsistence rice farming in the Ganges valley in India, an LEDC.

Can you answer this examination-style question?

Describe and explain the distribution of different farm types in the UK.

▶ Figure 1 The general distribution of the main farm types in England and Wales

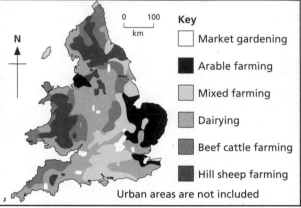

Key
- ☐ Market gardening
- ■ Arable farming
- ▨ Mixed farming
- ▨ Dairying
- ▨ Beef cattle farming
- ■ Hill sheep farming

Urban areas are not included

Farming in the UK

In the UK many farms are mixed farms but a general pattern (Figure 1) can be recognised:

	Arable farming	Dairying	Hill sheep farming	Market gardening
Definition	Growing of cereals, vegetables and animal feeds	Rearing of cattle for milk	Sheep rearing for meat and wool	Growing fruit, vegetables and flowers
Classification	Commercial, intensive, arable	Commercial, intensive, pastoral	Commercial, extensive, pastoral	Commercial, intensive, arable
Location	East and south east England, East Anglia	West of Britain and close to large cities	Upland areas of Britain, e.g. Pennines, Lake District	South and east of England and close to large cities
Physical factors	Flat relief; fertile well-drained soils; warm summers; rainfall – under 650mm (some in growing season); winter frosts to break up soil and kill pests	Gentle relief; fertile soils; high rainfall for grass growth; mild winters (over 6°C)	High, steep relief; thin infertile soils; high rainfall (over 1000 mm); low temperatures unsuitable for crops	Long hours of sunshine; most other factors are controlled
Human factors	Large market in south east; good transport networks; benefits from EU subsidies and intervention price	Access to large markets; milk subsidies up to the 1980s when quotas introduced	Remote from large markets; limited labour; EU subsidies and grants	Access to motorways and airports; large labour and capital input

Know your case study

Hill sheep farming in the Lake District, UK

In the upland areas of Britain, sheep farming is the main farming activity due to the difficult physical conditions and human factors. Breeds of hill sheep, e.g. the Swaledales, can survive the extremes of weather and poor quality pasture.

Hill sheep farming is an example of extensive commercial pastoral farming.

The farm as a system

Inputs		Processes	Outputs
Physical	**Human**		
Relief: uplands with steep slopes Soils: thin, rocky, acid and leached podsols Climate: 1°C fall in temperature every 160 metres. Short growing season. Over 2000mm rainfall on the fells	Market: small in local area Labour: little available in sparsely-populated uplands Capital: often little profit to reinvest Politics: subsidies and grants help some farmers to have a minimum standard of living Power and machinery, e.g. quad bikes	Lambing Shearing Dipping Fertilizing	Lambs for meat Wool fleeces Profit Money from bed and breakfast

Characteristics of a hill sheep farm

Three zones of land use:
- **the fell:** the tops of the hills over 300m altitude – sheep graze on this open land in the summer;
- **the intake or lower slopes:** divided into fields by dry stone walls, some pasture is improved by adding drainage and fertilizers;
- **the inbye:** the small area of land on the valley floor close to the farm buildings – more fertile soils and sheltered. Used for lambing, shearing etc. and for growing some winter fodder crops, e.g. turnips, hay.

Recent problems
- Hill sheep farming is not always profitable – the land is marginal.
- The threat of removal of subsidies from the European Union.
- Costs, e.g. fuel, machinery, fodder, have all risen but lamb prices in the late 1990s collapsed.
- Fewer young people want to carry on sheep farming.
- Conflicts with tourists and National Park Authorities.

Changes and improvements
- New breeding stock to improve quality and quantity of meat and wool.
- Greater use of fertilizers to improve quality of pasture.
- Grants for new farm buildings so lambing can be done indoors.
- EU subsidies and grants to encourage conservation of dry stone walls, natural pastures, stone barns, hedgerows.
- Diversification of farms, either farm-based, e.g. organic farming, rearing other animals (deer, goats), or non-farm based, e.g. camp-sites, sporting activities, forestry.
- Some farms could not survive and have been sold – often as second homes.

Test Yourself

Cover this page

Is hill sheep farming:
- commercial or subsistence
- arable or pastoral
- intensive or extensive?

Explain each of your answers.

Name an area where hill sheep farming takes place.

Draw a systems diagram for a hill sheep farm.

Describe the problems and changes faced by hill sheep farmers.

Know your case study

Flower and bulb growing in the Netherlands

The flower growing area lies in the west of the Netherlands, (Figure 1). This farm or flower holding is in Westland.

The farm as a system

Inputs	Processes	Outputs
22 000 square metres land Glasshouses Natural gas for heating Fertilizers, pesticides Sprinkler systems Fresh soil Computer technology 1-5 permanent workers Capital	Planting Watering Picking Weeding Fertilizing Spraying Packing	Cut flowers Bulbs Profit

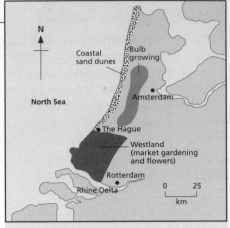

▲ *Figure 1: Location of Westland in the Netherlands*

Characteristics of market gardening and bulb growing
- The relief is low-lying and flat and both the soils and climate are artificially controlled inside the greenhouses.
- Most holdings are less than one hectare.
- Highly-intensive commercial form of farming – very high inputs of capital and labour, small land area and high outputs. It is a high-tech type of farming.
- In the Netherlands, co-operatives market the produce.
- Access to motorways and Schipol airport is important for export of the cut flowers because they are perishable.
- Farming is intensive because of the shortage of land; it needs to be profitable to compete with other land-uses.

Test Yourself

Draw the farm as a systems diagram.

Why are the physical conditions (relief, soils and climate) of Westland not important to the flower grower?

Explain how flower growing is both labour intensive and capital intensive.

Farming in LEDCs

Know your case study

Subsistence rice farming in the Ganges Valley, India

The Ganges valley is very densely populated and rice is the staple (main) food crop. Rice growing is an intensive and subsistence type of farming.

The farm as a system

Inputs	Processes	Outputs
Five month growing season Temperatures over21°C Monsoon rainfall over 2000mm Flat land to flood Dry time for harvesting Heavy alluvial or clay soils to provide an impervious layer Large labour force Water buffaloes for ploughing Rice seeds	Ploughing Planting Harvesting Threshing Weeding	Rice Manure for fertilizing Rice seeds

Problems of rice growing
- Flooding – provides water and fertile silt to grow the rice but sometimes disaster strikes when the floods are so severe that they destroy the rice crop.
- Drought – in some years the monsoon rains 'fail' and the rice crop is ruined.
- Shortage of land and a growing population – many patches of land are too small to support the family. The situation is made worse by the ever increasing population. Food shortages are a real problem.

Key Idea 3: agricultural change can have advantages and disadvantages in LEDCs

What you need to study and to learn:
- the Green Revolution has increased food production by using high yielding seeds, fertilizers and machinery but not all farmers have benefited;
- irrigation and soil conservation have helped increase food production;
- it is important that appropriate technology is used.

Changes to rice growing in the Ganges Basin

1 The Green Revolution:
- the use of HYVs or high yielding seed varieties, such as IR8, more than trebled food production, giving higher average yields and allowing double or treble cropping;
- greater use of fertilizers, tractors and mechanized ploughs;
- grants and loans to buy new seeds and equipment.

But there are both advantages and disadvantages:

Advantages	Disadvantages
Yields increased three times; Multiple cropping; Other crops grown which varied the diet; Surplus to sell in cities creating profit; Improving standard of living; Allows purchase of fertilizers, machinery.	Poor farmers could not afford HYVs, fertilizers and machinery; Some borrowed and ended up with large debts; HYVs need more water and fertilizer, which is expensive.

2 Irrigation
Despite the monsoon rains the water supply can be inadequate for growing rice, especially if more than one crop is grown. So irrigation is needed.

In the Ganges valley there are:
- wells: holes dug to reach underground water supplies, the water is lifted from the well using a shaduf or waterwheel or modern electric pumps – the water is then fed along open channels to the fields;
- inundation canals on the river banks which fill up as the river floods and take the water to the fields.

3 Appropriate technology
This is technology suited to the needs, skills, knowledge and wealth of the people. Large expensive irrigation projects and dams have many disadvantages. Appropriate technology is needed, for example,
- individual wells with easy to maintain, simple pumps
- renewable energy sources which use local resources, e.g. wind, solar power, biogas
- projects which use local labour rather than machinery
- no hi-tech machines needing expensive fuel and foreign spares
- low cost schemes which are sustainable.

4 Soil Conservation
To stop the erosion of top soil, conservation schemes are needed:
- to build terraces on sloping land
- to plant cover crops and windbreaks
- add manure and straw to soil.

Test Yourself

Cover this page. Write down four changes brought about by the Green Revolution. What are the advantages and disadvantages of the Green Revolution?

Describe one method of irrigation used in the Ganges Valley.

What are the characteristics of appropriate technology?

Describe one method of soil conservation.

Key Idea 3: agricultural change can have advantages and disadvantages in MEDCs

What you need to study and to know:
- in many MEDCs, hedge removal and modern farming practices have caused soil erosion;
- political influences, e.g. government, the EU, can affect farming;
- the EU, through the Common Agricultural Policy (CAP), uses quotas, set-aside schemes and subsidies to control farm production.

Hedge removal

This increases farm size and yields, and makes it easier to use large machinery. However, wildlife habitats are lost, soil erosion is increased and 'prairieization' occurs.

The Common Agricultural Policy (CAP)

The CAP has brought many changes to farming:

1 **Price support policies:** a target price is set for farm produce and also an intervention price. If the price of farm produce falls to the intervention price the EU buys the product. This guarantees a minimum price for the farmer but can lead to the EU building up food mountains.

2 **Subsidies:** this is money paid to farmers for producing certain crops, e.g. oil seed rape. They encourage the farmers to grow more of the subsidised crop making the EU more self-sufficient in many food-stuffs. But the drive to increase yields has led to:
   - the increased use of chemical fertilizers and pesticides,
   - the removal of hedgerows and woodlands,
   - greater soil erosion,
   - over-production, particularly of wheat, and huge grain mountains.

3 **Set-aside:** introduced in 1992 to stop over-production. Farmers are paid not to use at least 20 per cent of their arable land for 5 years.

4 **Quotas:** are used to control production, for example, to avoid butter mountains and milk lakes. Dairy farmers have to buy a quota which allows them to produce a maximum amount of milk.

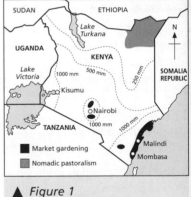

▲ *Figure 1*

Examination practice question

Study Figure 1 showing market gardening and nomadic pastoralism in Kenya.

(a) (i) Nomadic pastoralism is an example of subsistence farming. Explain the meaning of subsistence farming. (2 marks)

    (ii) Market gardening is an example of intensive farming. Explain the meaning of intensive farming. (2 marks)

    (iii) Using Figure 1, describe the distribution of market gardening in Kenya. (2 marks)

    (iv) Explain the benefits of market gardening to a LEDC such as Kenya. (4 marks)

(b) Choose an example of commercial farming you have studied.

    (i) Give the type of farming and its location. (1 mark)

    (ii) Explain the physical and human factors which encourage this type of farming in the location you have studied. (8 marks)

(c) (i) What is the meaning of the term 'irrigation'? (1 mark)

    (ii) Name and describe one method by which land can be irrigated. (2 marks)

    (iii) Explain the advantages of irrigation for the farmer. (3 marks)

[Check your answers on page 125-6] Total = 25 marks

Summary

Key words from the syllabus

arable	labour	relief
capital	irrigation	shifting cultivation
commercial	market	soil
dairying	market gardening	soil conservation
extensive	monoculture	soil erosion
farm system	pastoral nomadism	subsidies
Green Revolution	plantation	subsistence farming
hill sheep	politics	yields
intensive	quotas	

Test Yourself

Write down a definition for each of the key words. Check them with those given on page 78.

Check-list for revision

	Understand and know	Need more revision	Do not understand	Hints and tips
I can produce a systems diagram for a farm	☐	☐	☐	p 146
I know three physical and human factors which affect farming	☐	☐	☐	p 147
I know the general distribution of farm types in Britain	☐	☐	☐	p 148
I can explain the distribution of dairying, arable, hill sheep and market gardening in Britain	☐	☐	☐	pp 148-9
I know what the Green Revolution is and its advantages and disadvantages	☐	☐	☐	p 163
I know the advantages of appropriate technology in LEDCs	☐	☐	☐	p 164
I know how the CAP in the EU has affected agriculture	☐	☐	☐	pp 152, 156
I know the causes and effects of soil erosion and hedge removal in MEDCs	☐	☐	☐	p 153

Hints and Tips!

The page numbers refer to where the topic can be found in your text book *Understanding GCSE Geography*. If you don't understand the topic read the relevant section in your text book, make some notes and learn about it.

Test Yourself

Tick the boxes and fill in the gaps – if you still do not understand seek help from your teacher.

Know your case studies

Which real places have you studied as an example of...

● commercial farming	name:_____	pp 151, 154, 157, 160
● subsistence farming	name:_____	pp 158-9, 162
● intensive farming	name:_____	pp 151, 157, 160
● extensive farming	name:_____	p 154

I know a case study of:

● irrigation in an LEDC	name:_____	p 163
● the Green Revolution	name:_____	p 163
● appropriate technology	name:_____	p 164
● soil erosion and conservation	name:_____	p 161

11 Industry

Exam Watch

Key Ideas
1 Industrial activity can be classified into four types.
2 Industry is a system.
3 Many factors influence where an industry is located.
4 Industry changes over time.

A question on this topic appears in your second written paper. It is a 25 mark question and it will be Question 4.

You answer this question or the question on Agriculture.

Key words and definitions

footloose industry	light industries which have considerable freedom in location
greenfield site	rural land not previously built on in an out-of-town location
hi-tech industries	advanced modern industries which depend upon research
industrial estate	area in which several manufacturing companies have their factories
multi-nationals	large companies with business interests in many different countries
Newly Industrializing Countries (NICs)	LEDCs in which manufacturing industries have grown leading to economic development
primary industry	those which extract raw materials from land and sea
quaternary industry	high-technology research-based industries
science parks	areas where high-technology research companies are located, linked to a university
secondary industries	industries which process raw materials to make other products
tertiary industries	those which provide services to people and to other industries

Key Idea 1: industrial activity can be classified into four types

What you need to study and to know:
In the table below are examples of the four types of industry. The relative importance of these different types of industry is a good indicator of whether a country is a MEDC or a LEDC.

Test Yourself

Type of industry	Examples	
Primary	Mining, quarrying, logging, farming and fishing	
Secondary	Making petrol and plastics by refining crude oil. Making flour from wheat	
Tertiary	Shops and offices Health and education	Tourism and leisure Transport
Quaternary	Development and design of computers, micro-processors and telecommunications equipment	

Cover the definitions.

Check that you know them.

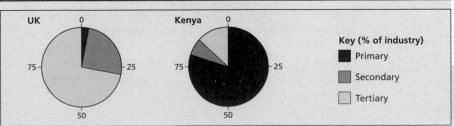

Key (% of industry)
■ Primary
▬ Secondary
□ Tertiary

◀ Figure 1 Industry in the UK, a MEDC, and Kenya, a LEDC

Key Idea 2: industry is a system

What you need to study and to know:
Figure 2 shows what is meant by the factory as a system.

Example – a steelworks:
- main input is iron ore, a raw material mined from the ground.
- main process is heating the iron ore to such high temperatures that it melts.
- main output is steel products, such as girders or rails or sheets for sale to other companies.

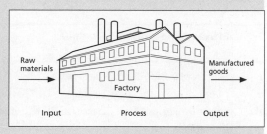

▲ *Figure 2 A simple factory system*

To be profitable, the value of the outputs from the factory must be greater than the costs of the inputs plus all the costs of processing them (energy, work force, equipment etc.). Notice another output shown on Figure 3 – waste. This is a problem for many heavy industries and the cost of disposing of it or making it safe have to be paid by the company running the factory

However, the system is often more complicated than this. Look at Figure 3.

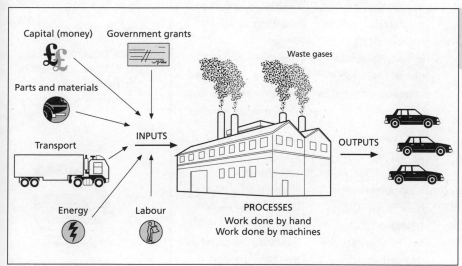

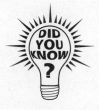

◀ *Figure 3 A more complex factory system*

For example, there are a great number of different inputs for a car factory. These are described in more detail below.
- capital – money invested by the company to build the works, buy the machines etc.
- government grants – money to help the company because of the large number of jobs created
- parts – bodies, engines, wheels, windscreens etc. and materials – paint, oil etc.
- transport – costs of bringing in the parts by road
- energy – power to run the assembly line machinery etc.
- labour force – people with a mixture of skills

Inputs have a big influence upon the location chosen for a factory.

Heavy industry

Steel is an example of a heavy industry.

Other heavy industries are oil refining and engineering.

They are large scale industries.

They cover large areas of land.

They make large or bulky products.

Light industry

Light industries are the opposite of heavy industries.

They are small-scale industries.

They can locate on industrial estates.

They make products people can buy.

Examples are electrical goods and food processing equipment.

Key Idea 3: many factors influence where a factory is located

What you need to study and to know:

Four of the most important factors which affect the choice of location for a factory are given in the table below. Their relative importance varies from industry to industry.

Factor for location	Definition	Effects on location	Examples
Raw materials	Materials from which goods are made, e.g. metals, wood, farm products. Often heavy and may be needed in large amounts	Factories which use many raw materials, often heavy industries, are located near them or on the coast for cheap import by sea	Steelworks are coastal, e.g. Teesside, because all the iron ore used is imported. Sugar factories are located in farming regions where sugar beet is grown, e.g. East Anglia and around York
Energy	Fuel and power, such as coal, oil, gas and electricity. Needed for heat and to drive machinery	Factories which use large amounts of energy, usually heavy industries, like to locate close to the source. Light industries, which use electricity, have more freedom of location	Many heavy industries were located next to coalfields, e.g. metal smelting in South Wales. The many light industries in the M4 corridor are not near local energy sources
Labour	What may be important is the cost of labour, or the skills of the workers, or numbers of workers available	For labour-intensive industries, e.g. textiles, cheap labour is important. For hi-tech industries, highly-educated skilled workers are needed most	Local universities and research establishments supply some of the skilled workforce for the many hi-tech industries located in the M4 corridor between Bristol and London
Transport	Road, rail, sea and air. Movement of raw materials and energy supplies to the factory. Movement of manufactured goods to market	Often more important for heavy industries because of their high raw material needs. Light industries are more interested in goods reaching market quickly	Oil refineries are located on the coast, e.g. Teesside, because crude oil is most cheaply transported by supertanker. Light industries are often located next to motorways, e.g. industrial estates next to the M4 in Reading

The three main types of secondary (manufacturing) industries are:

- heavy;
- light (or consumer);
- hi-tech.

Light and hi-tech can be combined under one heading:

- footloose.

Footloose means that industries have a lot of freedom in choosing a location.

Which factors affect the location of:

(a) heavy industries?

(b) light industries?

There are other factors which affect industrial location.
- capital – money invested in the factory building and machinery inside it. The larger the factory, the greater the investment needed.
- government – it may use grants and cheap loans to attract an industry to an area, often an area with high rates of unemployment.
- market – if the goods manufactured are large and heavy, such as steel, a location near to the market, or on the coast for cheap sea transport, is essential. If the goods are perishable, such as bread and cakes, they need a location next to a fast transport link, such as a motorway.

When an owner finds what should be a profitable location for the factory, the final factor to consider is site – i.e. where exactly will the factory be built? For light industries any industrial estate is often good enough and there is plenty of choice; for heavy industries a large area of cheap and unused flat land is needed, which restricts choice.

Know your case study

Heavy industry on Teesside
Key facts:
- industries – steel, chemicals, oil refining;
- factors for growth:

A – in the past:
local raw materials	– iron ore, salt and gypsum
local energy	– coal from the Durham coalfield
local market	– for steel in the shipyards.

B – today:
transport	– the Tees estuary is wide, deep and sheltered
	– large bulk carriers bring iron ore
	– supertankers bring crude oil
labour supply	– long history of working in these industries
site	– large areas of flat unused land around the Tees estuary.

Test Yourself

Cover up these two pages.

Can you name all eight factors for the location of industry?

Hints and Tips!
Practise drawing sketch maps.

Label them to suit the question.

How many of the key points have been labelled on Figure 1?

They can help you to revise and remember key points.

Drawing a good sketch map in the exam can gain you high marks.

Hints and Tips!
For a case study, there's no need to know a great mass of information.

Select and learn the key points.

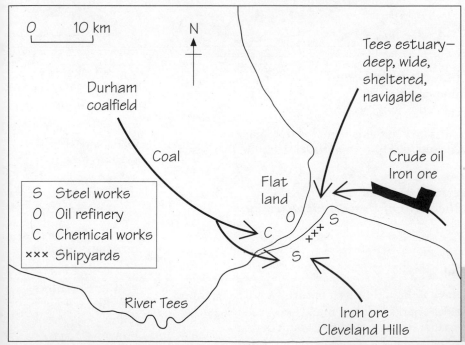

◄ Figure 1 Sketch map: factors for the location of heavy industry on Teesside

Know your case study

Footloose industries in the M4 corridor
Key facts:
- industries – food processing, electrical and electronic goods, telecommunications equipment.
- factors for growth:

transport – next to the M4, near to Heathrow airport, on the high speed rail link between London and Bristol

market – the wealthiest and largest market in the country is concentrated in Greater London and surrounding counties
– motorway connections to the rest of Britain from the M4 and M25

skilled labour – popular area to live (near London, Heathrow and pleasant countryside) to attract skilled workers
– many University cities supply graduates (e.g. London, Oxford, Bristol, Reading)

Hints and Tips!

Learn about one industrial estate or business park as a short case study.

Don't be afraid to use an example from your own local area.

Test Yourself

Figure 1 is an outline sketch map of the M4 corridor

Add labels to Figure 1 which would be useful for explaining the growth of industries there.

◄ *Figure 1 The M4 corridor*

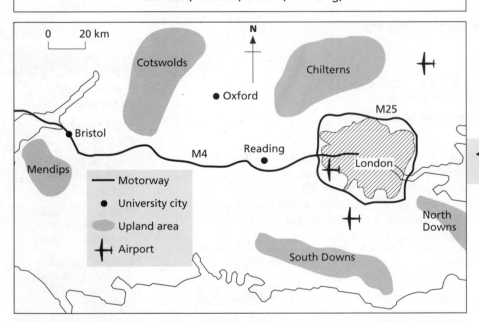

Key Idea 4: industry changes over time
What you need to study and to know:

A Changes within the UK
In 1900 heavy industries located on coalfields were the dominant industries. Approaching 2000 light and hi-tech industries are the thriving industries.

Two main changes in location have occurred.
1 From the inner city to the edges of the city attracted by:
- cheaper land
- more space
- closer to motorways
- more pleasant environment.

The edge of city locations, where light and hi-tech industries are to be found on industrial estates and business parks, are greenfield sites. Science parks are attached to universities, so that research and successful business opportunities can be linked together, and also use greenfield sites.

The old inner city locations are called brownfield sites.

The government wants industries to locate on them instead of on greenfield sites.

Can you think of reasons why the government wants this?

Why are industries likely to be less enthusiastic about brownfield sites?

2 *From the coalfield regions of northern and western parts of Britain to the south and east of England attracted by:*
- wealthy concentrated market
- motorways radiate out from London to all parts of Britain
- closest to the markets in the EU.

Often the only way to attract industries to the old coalfield regions is for the government to give financial help to new industries to locate there.

B Changes in the rest of the world

The most significant change in world industry over the last thirty years has been the growth of industry in East Asia. Less economically developed countries in which manufacturing industry has grown are called Newly Industrializing Countries or NICS for short.

The greatest advantage of East Asia is its **cheap labour** force. Figure 2 shows some of the wage rates in some of the countries there. The workers are well educated, reliable, hard working and there are many of them.

Under $1	Under $2	Under $5	Under $8	Over $12	Over $20
China	Philippines Indonesia	Thailand Malaysia	Singapore South Korea Hong Kong Taiwan	UK USA	Germany

Other advantages are:
- transport – these countries are close to the main shipping lanes; costs of moving manufactured goods long distances by sea have come down now that they can be put in containers.
- markets – even though many of the goods are for export, home markets are also increasing as people become wealthier.
- government – most have welcomed multi-national companies setting up factories in their countries.

Know your case study

Growth of industry in South Korea (an example of a NIC)

Key facts:
- industries – shipbuilding, steel, cars, electronics.
- companies – Samsung, Hyundai, LG and Daewoo.
- location – mostly in and around Seoul, the capital city.
- factors for growth:

labour	– a cheap and efficient workforce willing to work long hours
transport	– being a peninsula, everywhere is close to the sea
markets	– main overseas markets are around the Pacific, such as the USA and Japan
	– the big Korean companies have actively searched for overseas markets
government	– puts trade barriers up against imported manufactured goods, which keeps the home market for Korean companies.

Examples of NICs in East Asia are Hong Kong, Singapore, Taiwan, South Korea, Thailand and Malaysia.

Examples in other parts of the world are Brazil and Mexico.

◀ *Figure 2 Wage rates – average hourly rate in US dollars (1997)*

Containers are standard-sized boxes in which goods can be packed and locked away in the factory. They are easy to move between ship, lorry and train.

Test Yourself

Cover the page.

Name and explain the four factors for industrial growth in East Asia.

Memorise the key facts for South Korea.

C Industry is becoming more global

The main reason is the growth of multi-national corporations. These are:
- very large companies;
- with businesses in many different countries;
- with their headquarters usually located in a MEDC.

Examples are:

Name of company	Country with the HQ	Business interests
ICI	UK	Chemicals
Ford	USA	Motor vehicles
Nestle	Switzerland	Food and drinks
Sony	Japan	Electrical and electronic goods

They will set up factories and market their goods in a country anywhere in the world, provided they can make a profit. Improved communications of all kinds – air travel, container ships, satellite links, e-mail – has helped greatly. As usual, there are both benefits and problems.

Advantages of multi-nationals	Disadvantages of multi-nationals
They set up businesses that the country can't do for itself	They are doing it for their own gain and any profits made are exported out of the host country
They create jobs: light industries, e.g. textiles, may use a lot of labour	They may pay low wages and exploit the local workers
They bring other benefits such as improving transport and services	They can have poor safety records and are responsible for pollution
They increase exports to markets worldwide	Only a limited range of products are exported at the choice of the company rather than the country

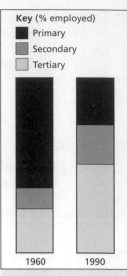

Key (% employed)
- ■ Primary
- ▨ Secondary
- ▢ Tertiary

▲ Figure 1
Employment in Malaysia

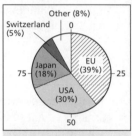

▲ Figure 2 Where the biggest multi-nationals are based

Examination practice question

(a) Name one example of each of the following industries:

    (i) primary;   (ii) secondary;   (iii) tertiary.   (3 marks)

(b) Figure 1 shows employment in Malaysia in 1960 and 1990.

    (i) From Figure 1, describe the changes in employment between 1960 and 1990.   (4 marks)

    (ii) Explain how the changes suggest that Malaysia had become more economically developed by 1990.   (2 marks)

(c) Malaysia is an example of one of the NICs in East Asia.

    (i) What do the letters NIC stand for?   (1 mark)

    (ii) Give the reasons why so much industrial growth has occurred in East Asian countries in the last thirty years.   (6 marks)

(d) Figure 2 shows where the headquarters of the largest multi-national corporations are located.

    (i) What is the evidence from Figure 2 that most multi-nationals have their headquarters in MEDCs?   (2 marks)

    (ii) With the help of one or more examples, explain the disadvantages of multi-national companies.   (7 marks)

[Check your answers on page 126]   Total: 25 marks

Summary

Key words from the syllabus

footloose industry	primary industry
greenfield site	quaternary industry
hi-tech industry	science park
industrial estate	secondary industry
multi-nationals	tertiary industry
Newly Industrializing Countries	

Test Yourself

Write down a definition for each of the key words. Check them with those given on page 86.

Checklist for revision

	Understand and know	Need more revision	Do not understand	Hints and tips
I know the names of the four types of industry	☐	☐	☐	pp 166-7
I can explain industry as a system	☐	☐	☐	p 168
I can name examples of footloose industries	☐	☐	☐	p 169
I can give five factors which affect industrial location	☐	☐	☐	pp 170-1
I can explain why raw materials affect the location of heavy industries more than light industries	☐	☐	☐	pp 170-1
I understand why labour is an important locational factor for hi-tech industries	☐	☐	☐	p 174
I can name some characteristics of multi-nationals	☐	☐	☐	pp 178-9
I know some of the advantages and disadvantages of multi-nationals	☐	☐	☐	p 179
I can explain why many NICs are in East Asia	☐	☐	☐	p 180
I can state the difference between a brownfield and a greenfield site	☐	☐	☐	p 182
I know the advantages and disadvantages of greenfield sites	☐	☐	☐	p 182

Hints and Tips!

The page numbers refer to where the topic can be found in your text book *Understanding GCSE Geography*. If you don't understand the topic read the relevant section in your text book, make some notes and learn about it.

Test Yourself

Tick the boxes and fill in the gaps – if you still do not understand seek help from your teacher.

Know your case studies

Which real places have you studied as an example of...
- an industrial area in the UK   name:_____   pp 174-5
- a Newly Industrializing Country (a LEDC)   name:_____   p 181

12 Managing resources and tourism

Key Ideas
1 Mangement of resources is crucial to sustainable development.
2 Environments offer possibilities for tourism and development.
Each key idea will be looked at in turn.

A question on this topic appears in your second written paper.

It is a 25 mark question and it will be Question 5.

You answer this question or the question on Development and interdependence.

Key words and definitions

acid rain	pollutants in the atmosphere which are deposited on the Earth's surface when it rains
alternative energy sources	sources of heat and power which can be used instead of fossil fuels
fossil fuels	sources of heat such as coal, oil and natural gas
finite resources	those which exist in limited amounts; once used up, they are no more
global warming	the theory that the average temperature of the Earth is rising as a result of higher concentrations of carbon dioxide in the atmosphere
green tourism	tourism in which protection of the environment and of the way of life of local people are considered very important. Also called eco-tourism
National Park	an area of beautiful scenery which is managed for conservation and for visitors
non-renewable resources	resources that can be used only once and are then used up
ozone layer damage	hole in the layer of ozone gas high in the atmosphere
recycling	recovery of waste products to be converted into materials which can be used again
renewable resources	those which are naturally replaced after use and don't run out
sustainable development	activities and economic growth with a good future because the environment upon which they depend is not being destroyed

Key Idea 1: management of resources is crucial to sustainable development

What you need to study and to know:
- The Earth provides us with many natural resources, but more are needed.
- Those that come from the atmosphere, such as light, heat, water and wind, are renewable.
- However, some of those which come from the ground, such as coal, oil and natural gas, are non-renewable. When burnt there will be no replacements for hundreds of millions of years.
- Yet, the world depends for its energy supplies on these non-renewable fossil fuels.
- In addition, total world energy consumption continues to increase.

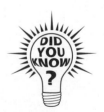

The current life expectancies of fossil fuels:

coal = 240 years;
gas = 70 years;
oil = 45 years.

There are two good reasons why the demand for energy will keep on growing.

1 **Population growth** – more and more people on the Earth. There are now over six billion of us. Look at Figure 1 which shows that the number of years for the total world population to increase by one billion is getting less and less. This must increase demand for natural resources.

2 **Economic development** – as people in LEDCs become more wealthy, they want to enjoy the same quality of life as people in MEDCs. People in the countryside in LEDCs hope for electricity – then they can run a fridge (of great importance in hot countries) and a TV (to watch sport, soaps and films just like you do). People in the towns in LEDCs hope for a car and a computer giving them access to the Internet. Figure 2 illustrates how low energy consumption is per head in LEDCs. If the four billion plus people living in LEDCs become just slightly better off, there will be a massive increase in energy demand.

Conservation of resources and the need to find alternatives

Not only is there a need to prepare for a time when fossil fuels will run out, but it is also desirable that we reduce environmental damage, much of it caused by burning fossil fuels. Figure 3 suggests that people are ruining the environment in a big way. Burning fossil fuels, particularly coal, is blamed for causing global warming and acid rain. Release of chemicals, particularly those containing CFCs that were used in fridges and aerosol sprays, caused the hole in the ozone layer. These are international problems; getting countries to agree to measures for reducing pollution isn't easy.

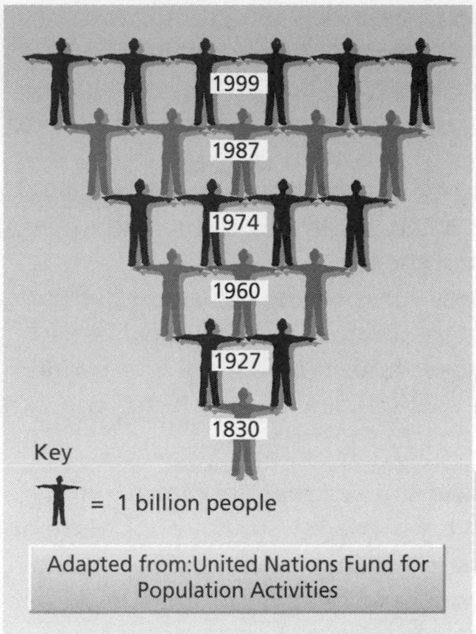
1999
1987
1974
1960
1927
1830
Key
= 1 billion people
Adapted from:United Nations Fund for Population Activities

Test Yourself

In what ways does your family consume energy?

Has your family's consumption of energy increased in the last ten years?

◀ *Figure 1 Total world population*

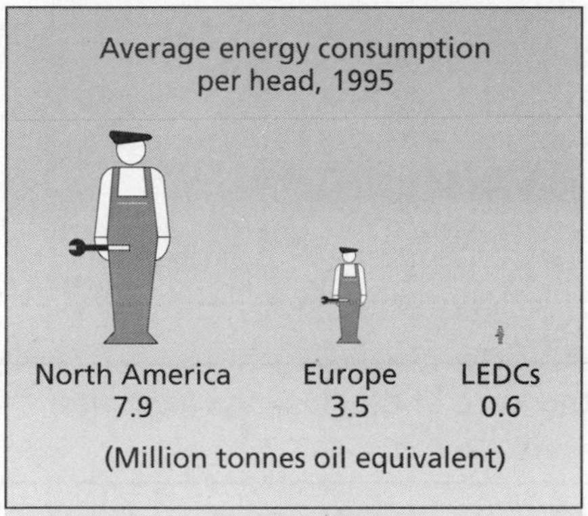
Average energy consumption per head, 1995
North America
7.9
Europe
3.5
LEDCs
0.6
(Million tonnes oil equivalent)

▲ *Figure 2 Average energy consumption per head 1995*

DID YOU KNOW?

There are international agreements to reduce pollution:

1 The Montreal Protocol – for the ozone hole
- phase out CFCs and halons by 2000

2 EU Directives – for acid rain
- reduce emissions of sulphur dioxide by 60 per cent by 2003
- reduce emissions of oxides of nitrogen by 75 per cent

3 Climate Change Summit in Japan – for global warming
- MEDCs to cut CO_2 emissions by 5 per cent by 2012

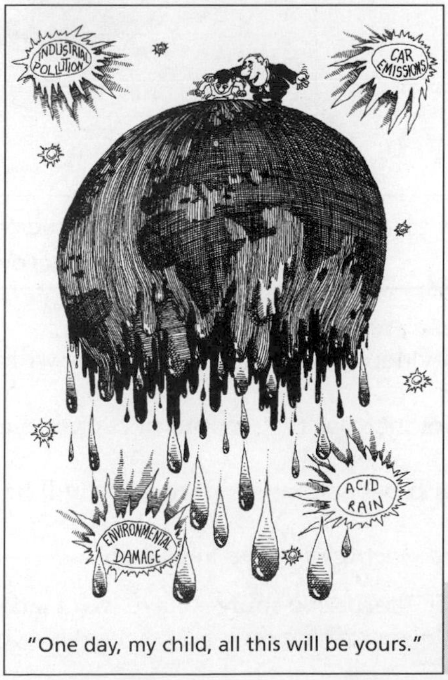
INDUSTRIAL POLLUTION
CAR EMISSIONS
ACID RAIN
ENVIRONMENTAL DAMAGE
"One day, my child, all this will be yours."

◀ *Figure 3 Consequences of burning fossil fuels*

There are some ways in which non-renewable resources can be conserved.

- Recycling – making used products into new materials. This is done for scrap metals, aluminium cans, glass bottles and old clothes. This reduces the amount of non-renewable resources such as iron ore and bauxite that need to be mined.
- Reducing energy consumption – saving electricity by switching off lights and electrical equipment when not in use, or by walking, biking or using the bus and train instead of the car.
- Increasing energy efficiency – improving the quality of buildings so that less heat is lost is one way of doing this. Using heat already given off by running machinery, e.g. greenhouses heated by warm water from power stations, or making more fuel-efficient planes, buses and cars, are other ways.

However, there is a limit to the amount that people are willing to conserve. How easy is it to persuade a car owner to use the bus? More hope is being pinned on developing alternative energy sources using resources from the atmosphere such as water, wind and heat. Some are shown in Figure 1.

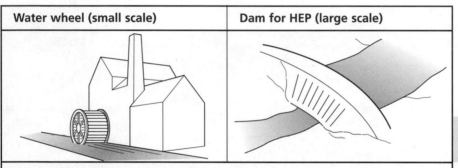

Water wheel (small scale)	Dam for HEP (large scale)
Electricity is generated by the force of the flowing water after the rainfall has been concentrated in rivers	
Wind turbine	Solar panel
Strong winds drive turbines to generate electricity	The sun's light is converted into electricity by PVs (photovoltaic cells)

The advantages of using these are:
- they are renewable as they depend on natural resources which are always going to be there;
- they are clean and will not increase the amount of carbon dioxide in the atmosphere;
- there are several different types so that every country will have at least one they can use;
- most can be used to make electricity in the local area.

Here is a question for you. 'If alternative sources have many advantages over fossil fuels, why did they contribute only 6.1 per cent to world energy consumption in 1996?'

How energy efficient is your home or your school?

How easy is it for heat to escape in winter through windows, walls and roofs?

Hints and Tips!

Never be afraid to use local/personal knowledge in your exam answers.

◀ *Figure 1 Alternative energy sources*

DID YOU KNOW?

Alternative energy sources are sustainable.

They use sun, wind and rain which should never run out.

Test Yourself

Cover the page.

Name the alternative sources.

List their advantages.

There are several reasons why fossil fuels remain more popular than the alternatives.

Reason	Fossil fuels	Alternative energy sources
Familiarity	People have used them for many years and they have many different uses	They are new and can only be used for making electricity (they are not fuels)
Cost	Oil and gas are very cheap to drill for and transport	Research is expensive and the cost of the electricity produced is greater than that from fossil fuels
Need	Fossil fuel supplies are still plentiful today	Research and development is less easy to justify without shortages

But what will be the cost of, and need for, fossil fuels be in 40 years time?

Petrol costs under 10 pence per litre in some countries which don't tax it.

Crude oil, once discovered, is a natural resource which can be obtained cheaply.

Know your case study

An alternative energy source

HEP (hydro-electric power)
Conditions needed for its production:
- fast-flowing water, e.g. a waterfall
- high rainfall spread throughout the year
- lake or deep valley which can be dammed.

Advantages and disadvantages:

Advantages	Disadvantages
• renewable • no pollution • cheaper electricity than from power stations	• suitable conditions are not found everywhere • often they are in sparsely populated areas • high cost of setting them up • dam building has bad effects on local people and the environment

Examples: – Aswan High Dam on the Nile; in the Scottish Highlands, e.g. near Fort William

Activity

1 In the following table, put a tick or cross in the boxes for fossil fuels, HEP and one other type of energy, as for wind power.

Factors for assessment	Fossil fuels	HEP	Wind power	One other
Renewable			✓	
Does not release carbon dioxide			✓	
Does not pollute the air			✓	
Does not cause local environmental problems			✗	
Cheap energy source			✓	
Long-known technology			✗	
Simple technology for use in remote areas in LEDCs			✓	
Always available – not reliant on the weather			✗	

Hints and Tips!

Look at page 126 for the answers to this Activity.

Key Idea 2: environments offer possibilities for tourism and development

What you need to study and to know:

Tourism is one of the service industries and it is growing fast. There are many types of environments which attract tourists.

1 **Sand and sea**, preferably where the climate is warm and sunny.

In the UK, the greatest number of resorts are along the south coast of England which has the warmest summers (17°C compared with 13°C in northern Scotland).

In Europe, the Mediterranean climate, with its hot (25°C), dry and sunny summers, attracts visitors to Spain, Greece, Italy and France.

Worldwide, the Caribbean or the Far East (Malaysia, Bali etc.) have temperatures around 30°C and eight hours sunshine in the middle of the British winter!

2 **Uplands and mountains**

In the UK, most of the National Parks of England and Wales were created in upland areas. Looking at the scenery and walking are the general tourist activities, but more specialised ones include rock climbing, sailing, pony trekking and potholing. In the Highlands of Scotland there is skiing as well.

In Europe, Alpine resorts in France, Switzerland, Austria and Italy offer both great winter skiing and excellent summer walking and sightseeing with views of glaciers and snow-capped peaks.

Worldwide, individual attractions, such as the Grand Canyon in the USA or the Victoria Falls in Zimbabwe, attract thousands of visitors each year.

3 **Special attractions**

Some of these are based on natural attractions, such as the wildlife in Africa's Game Parks. Others have human attractions as well, such as the Inca remains in Peru in the Andes mountains or the pyramids, temples and statues of the Nile valley in Egypt.

Hints and Tips!

Try to be specific when referring to temperatures in exam answers. Quote values as has been done here.

Hints and Tips!

Case studies

Prepare for the exam by writing down the key facts of two case studies.

1 A National Park in the UK: choose the one most familiar to you, e.g. the one nearest to where you live.

2 A tourist area in a LEDC.

Name and describe the attractions (physical and human) of each one.

▼ *Figure 1 Some popular destinations in LEDCs*

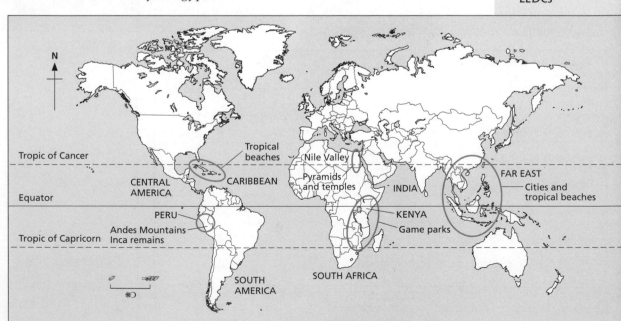

Many LEDCs export only a limited number of low-value primary products. These doesn't earn them much foreign exchange. However, if the country has environments attractive to tourists, the economy benefits in two ways:
- more foreign exchange income;
- a greater variety of ways of earning income.

There are also benefits to local people in tourist areas:
- service sector jobs are created in hotels, cafes, transport etc;
- farmers have a market for their food products;
- craft industries develop to satisfy the demand for souvenirs;
- improved services – roads, water and electricity supplies – are provided;
- more jobs exist so that fewer people are forced to migrate to the big cities for work.

Tourism creates problems.

There are three types of problems:
- environmental;
- conflicts between visitors and local people;
- economic.

These headings can be used for all tourist areas, but the exact nature of the problems will vary.

Cover the page. Check that you know the benefits and problems of tourism:
(a) to the country,
(b) to local people.

Hints and Tips!

Extend your two case studies by describing for each one:

(a) the benefits
(b) the problems of tourism.

Know your case study

Problems in a National Park in the UK

Environmental problems:
- pressure on landscapes frequently visited, e.g. footpath erosion
- litter pollution.

Conflicts:
- between visitors and farmers caused by tourists leaving gates open, letting dogs loose at lambing times etc.
- between visitors and villagers caused by traffic congestion, bad parking and noise.

Economic problems:
- visitor numbers rise and fall during the year
- tourist jobs are badly paid and seasonal.

Know your case study

Problems in Kenya, a LEDC example

Environmental problems:
- destruction of the natural environment and habitats by building airports, roads and hotels for tourists
- pressure on landscapes from many mini-buses in popular game viewing areas
- destruction of coral reefs.

Conflicts between tourists and local people caused by:
- farmland being taken away for game parks
- crops being eaten or flattened by the wild animals on farms near the parks
- a few local people earning money from tourist visitors.

Economic problems:
- visitor numbers have gone down in recent years
- most jobs created by tourism are badly paid
- people are out of work when the tourists don't come.

Management of tourist areas

National Parks are examples of tourist areas which are managed. Tourist management in these is a mixture of:

- being positive – promoting tourist use by providing facilities for visitors (information centres, car parks etc.), making and repairing footpaths, educating visitors about the country code;
- being negative – controlling where tourists can walk, blocking off some areas to cars, controlling new developments in and around farms and villages.

In LEDCs, green tourism can lead to good management but it is also two sided. It involves local people to ensure they gain more of the benefits, but there is also a great concern to protect the environment. In Kenya, for example, instead of big lodges, small tented camps have been set up. The advantages are:

- tourists can get closer to the wildlife;
- the Masai tribes people are paid a rent and used as workers;
- tourists in small groups do less environmental damage in the game parks.

Test Yourself

What is meant by sustainable tourism?

Hints and Tips!

Finish off your two case studies by describing methods of management in each one.

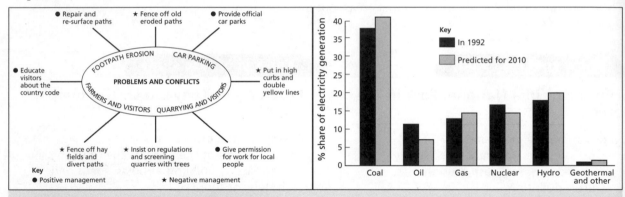

▲ Figure 1 Examples of National Park management methods

▲ Figure 2 Ways of making electricity in the world in 1992 and predicted for 2010

Examination practice question

(a) Look at Figure 2.

   (i) Name the fossil fuels used to make electricity. (1 mark)

   (ii) By what percentage is the use of coal expected to increase between 1992 and 2010? (1 mark)

(b) (i) Why are fossil fuels described as non-renewable resources? (2 marks)

   (ii) State two ways in which the increased use of coal for making electricity might cause further damage to the environment. (2 marks)

   (iii) Why is the world demand for electricity likely to increase over the next 50 years? (3 marks)

(c) Figure 2 shows that only a small increase in use of alternative energy sources is expected between 1992 and 2010. Give two reasons why the increase is likely to be so small. (4 marks)

(d) For one tourist area you have studied:

   (i) Name and locate it. (2 marks)

   (ii) Describe its environmental attractions for visitors. (3 marks)

   (iii) Explain the problems caused by tourism and the attempts made to reduce their effects. (7 marks)

[Check your answers on pages 126-7] Total: 25 marks

Summary

Key words from the syllabus	
acid rain	National Park
alternative energy sources	non-renewable
fossil fuels	ozone layer damage
finite resources	recycling
global warming	renewable energy
green tourism	sustainable development

Test Yourself

Write down a definition for each of the key words. Check them with those given on page 94.

Checklist for revision

	Understand and know	Need more revision	Do not understand	Hints and tips
I can name the fossil fuels	☐	☐	☐	p 187
I know why they are called non-renewable	☐	☐	☐	p 187
I understand the meaning of renewable energy sources	☐	☐	☐	p 186
I can name some examples of alternative energy sources	☐	☐	☐	pp 190-1
I know some advantages and disadvantages for alternative sources	☐	☐	☐	pp 191-2
I know what recycling is and can give an example	☐	☐	☐	p 194
I understand the meaning of energy efficiency	☐	☐	☐	p 194
I can name different types of places where tourists visit	☐	☐	☐	pp 198-9
I can describe the management methods used in National Parks	☐	☐	☐	pp 198, 201
I know some of the advantages and disadvantages of tourism for LEDCs	☐	☐	☐	p 206
I can explain how green tourism is different	☐	☐	☐	pp 206-7

Hints and Tips!

The page numbers refer to where the topic can be found in your text book *Understanding GCSE Geography*. If you don't understand the topic read the relevant section in your text book, make some notes and learn about it.

Test Yourself

Tick the boxes and fill in the gaps – if you still do not understand seek help from your teacher.

Know your case studies

Which real places have you studied as an example of...
- an alternative/renewable energy   name:_____   pp 192-3
- a National Park   name:_____   pp 200-2
- a tourist in a LEDC   name:_____   pp 203-5, 207

13 Development and interdependence

Key Ideas
1 Differences in the level of development between MEDCs and LEDCs are related to many factors – economic, environmental, social and political.
2 Interdependence between MEDCs and LEDCs in world trade means a shared responsibility.
Each key idea will be looked at in turn.

A question on this topic appears in your second written paper.

It is a 25 mark question and it will be Question 6.

You answer this question or the question on Managing resources and tourism.

Key words and definitions

aid	the transfer of money, goods and expertise from one country to another either free or at low cost
charitable aid	help given free from charities such as Oxfam
development	mainly measured by wealth which controls peoples' standards of living
GNP (Gross National Product)	total value of all the goods and services from a country in one year
hazard	a cause of damage to people and property such as a flood or earthquake
interdependence	when two countries have a shared need for each other's goods
long-term aid	help given with the aim of development for the future
political aid	government help usually given in the form of goods and services
product dependency	when a country relies on one or two products for most of its income
short-term aid	help given during and after an emergency such as food and medicines
tied aid	the country receiving help has to use the money to buy goods and services from the country giving the aid
trade	the exchange of goods and services between countries
trade grouping	several countries join together to remove barriers to the free movement of goods, such as the EU

Key Idea 1: differences in level of development between MEDCs and LEDCs are related to many factors – economic, environmental, social and political

What you need to study and to know:

You should be familiar with the North-South line on the world map (Figure 1). It separates MEDCs from LEDCs.

D stands for Developed

- Being economically developed means that a country is wealthy. Standards of living are high. Many people can afford cars, have a wide range of electrical goods in their homes and take at least one holiday a year.

Chapter 8 has more information on population data.

Figure 1 on page 86 gives employment differences between a MEDC and a LEDC

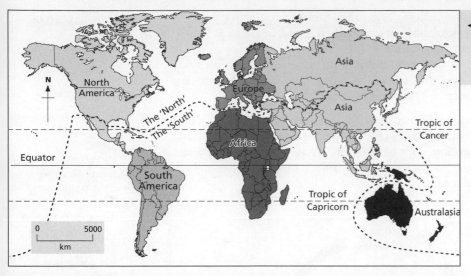

◀ *Figure 1 The world split into more and less economically developed countries*

> ● Being less economically developed means that, by world standards, a country is poor. The country will not be without rich people, but for many life is a struggle – just to find sufficient food to stay alive.

Hints and Tips!

It is essential that you know the names and locations of the continents.

These are needed when describing what a world map shows.

Note the positions of the Equator and Tropics on Figure 1.

Sometimes it is useful to use latitude as well.

The most important factor used to measure a country's level of development is GNP. It is calculated by:
(a) adding up the values of all the goods and services produced in a country during the year;
(b) dividing the total by the number of people living in the country.

GNP is used to compare the wealth of countries, which means it is an economic factor. Other factors, such as population characteristics, health and education, are about people, which makes them social factors. When it is difficult to separate the two, the term 'socio-economic' is used.

Some of the most widely used factors for measuring development are listed in the table below.

Hints and Tips!

Try to quote examples of actual values (as in the table below) in your examination answers. This makes them more precise.

Factors		Typical values for the:	
		richest MEDCs	poorest LEDCs
Economic:	GNP: Gross National Product per head (US$)	over 20 000	under 200
	Consumption of electricity per head	over 5 000	under 50
Social: Population	Birth rate per 1000 per year	10-15	over 40
	Rate of natural increase per year	under 1%	over 3%
	Population doubling time (years)	over 100	under 30
Health	Infant mortality rate	under 10	over 100
	Access to safe water	100%	under 50%
Education	Adult literacy rate	99%	under 33%
Socio-economic:	Televisions per 1000 people	over 400	under 20

It is difficult to collect reliable data for any of the factors measuring differences in levels of development between MEDCs and LEDCs.
- Some parts of LEDCs are very remote.
- Many people cannot read and write to fill in forms.
- Subsistence farmers use size of their herds rather than money to measure wealth which doesn't help in calculating the GNP!

Many factors are inter-related, although the basic reason for lack of development is usually economic, i.e. poverty. Social problems follow from it and cycles of poverty develop. Two of these are shown in Figure 1. Once established, these cycles become vicious circles from which it is extremely difficult for people to break out.

Test Yourself

Without turning back over the page
(a) name the six continents,
(b) name the three continents with most of the LEDCs,
(c) name five factors of development,
(d) give typical values for each of the five.

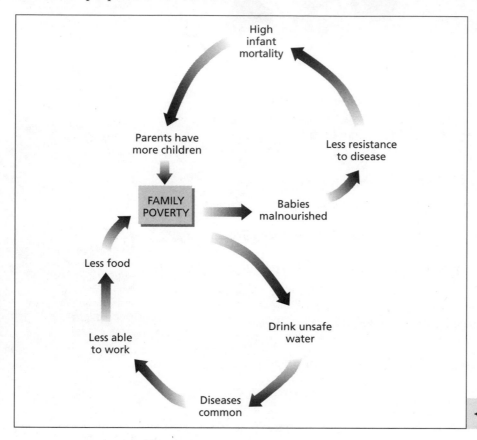

Figure 1 Poverty cycles

Test Yourself

Look carefully at the poverty cycles.

Draw one beginning 'Family poverty' → 'Little education' →

Note that in both cycles disease is mentioned. The poverty cycles highlight the two main causes of poor health for people in LEDCs:
- being malnourished (usually from being under-fed)
- having to drink unsafe (unclean) water.

As many LEDCs are located in the tropics, hot weather in the wet season gives ideal conditions for insects and bacteria to thrive and multiply. In rural areas in LEDCs only a tiny proportion of houses have a tap with safe water. Often people take water for drinking direct from rivers without any treatment. And the rivers are used for many different purposes! Fever and sickness from water-borne diseases, making people too weak to work, and killing infants and children, are frequent. One of the best ways an aid programme can help people in rural areas of the tropics is by providing pumps and pipes for clean water, and separating drinking water from water used for other purposes.

DID YOU KNOW?

Diseases spread by drinking or washing food in contaminated water are:
- diarrhoea
- dysentery
- cholera
- typhoid
- hepatitis.

Know your case study

A tropical disease – malaria

Areas affected
The main areas are shown in Figure 2.

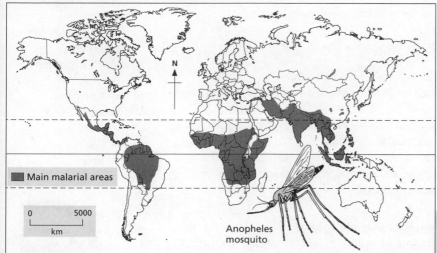

Main malarial areas

0   5000
km

Anopheles
mosquito

◀ *Figure 2 Areas most at risk from malaria*

Hints and Tips!

Describe the distribution of malaria.

When describing a distribution, you can also refer to areas where malaria isn't found, e.g. in temperate regions such as Europe and North America.

Causes
It is carried from an infected person by female anopheles mosquitoes. The mosquito bites another person who is then infected with the disease.
Mosquitoes breed in stagnant surface water and are most active at night.
People are most likely to be bitten and infected at night in the wet season.

Effects
At best, regular bouts of fever preventing work; at worst, death.

Prevention
Spray the breeding grounds.
Sleep under mosquito nets.
Keep skin covered by clothes at night.

Volcano

Flood

Earthquakes

Drought and famine

Tropical storms

▲ *Figure 3 Percentage loss of life from the five main natural hazards (1969 – 1993)*

Environmental hazards which contribute to lack of development

The main environmental hazards which cause damage and kill people are named in Figure 3. This gives some idea of their relative importance.

The ways in which these hazards affect people have already been covered in earlier chapters.

Hints and Tips!

Check the physical topics you are studying.

If you are not studying tectonic activity, rivers or weather, you will need to look back at the page numbers given.

Hazard	Page	Case study
Earthquake	11	Kobe, Japan, 1995
Volcano	10	Montserrat in the Caribbean, 1995-7
Flood	28	Mississippi, USA, 1993
Drought and famine	48	Drought in Ethiopia, 1983-4
Tropical storm	49	Hurricane Georges, September 1998

Key Idea 2: interdependence between MEDCs and LEDCs in world trade means a shared responsibility

What you need to study and to know:

Trade is the exchange of goods and services between countries. More than half the world's trade takes place between just seven countries, known as the G7, which includes some of the world's most wealthy and industrialized countries. Why?

- Being industrialized countries, they need lots of raw materials and energy supplies.
- They make a wide variety of manufactured goods.
- People can afford to eat foods or buy goods not produced in their own countries.
- Trade groupings, such as the EU, encourage trade by making it easy to cross borders without paying customs duties.
- Transport links have improved, e.g. motorways, high speed trains and tunnels link EU countries together, making for quicker and easier movement of goods between countries.

If you need to explain why there is little trade between countries (e.g. in Africa), use the opposites for the bullet points given for the G7 countries, such as:

- not much manufacturing industry;
- many are poor farmers;
- no trading groupings;
- poor or non-existent communications.

The basic feature of the pattern of world trade is illustrated in Figure 1.

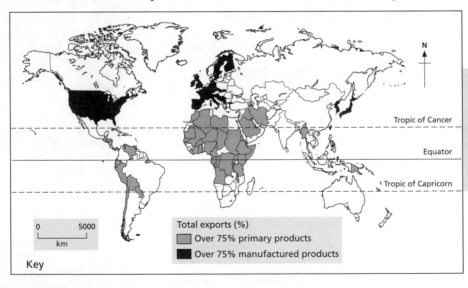

The G7 countries which dominate world trade are
- USA
- Germany
- Japan
- France
- UK
- Italy
- Canada.

Add labels to Figure 1 for the names of countries and continents which illustrate the key features of the pattern of world trade.

◀ *Figure 1 World export trade; countries with the greatest dependence on exporting manufactured goods and primary products*

90%+ crude oil from Nigeria and Saudi Arabia

80%+ copper from Zambia

60%+ coffee from Ethiopia

▲ *Figure 2 Examples of dependency on one export commodity*

From Figure 1, note that:
- the countries which rely most upon exporting manufactured goods are MEDCs (Japan, USA, European countries). Which is the only LEDC for which manufactured goods make up over 75 per cent of its exports?
- the countries which rely most upon exporting primary products are LEDCs, especially those in Africa and the Middle East. What is worse, they often have high product dependency, i.e. they rely upon the export of just one or two commodities.

MEDCs have many factories which need raw materials and fuels. LEDCs have many raw materials and fuels, but few industries and manufactured goods.

Therefore, MEDCs and LEDCs should be inter-dependent, i.e. they should depend upon each other, because each can supply what the other doesn't have. They need to trade.

- If MEDCs and LEDCs depend upon one another, trade between them should be in balance (Figure 3A). The real situation is shown in Figure 3B.

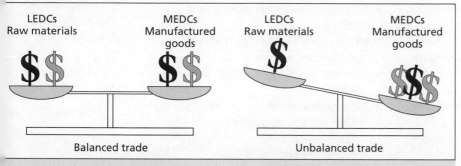

▲ Figure 3A Balanced trade   ▲ Figure 3B Unbalanced trade

Why does the pattern of world trade favour MEDCs?

Primary products (LEDCs)	Manufactured goods (MEDCs)
A Low in price	Sell at high prices
B Prices go up and down	Prices tend to move upwards only
C Output may go down, e.g. crops destroyed by bad weather	Markets in home country are protected by tariffs on imports

Aid

This is the transfer of money, goods and know-how from one country (the giver) to another (the receiver).

Types of aid

1 Bilateral – two sided aid, usually arranged between governments, which makes it political aid. It is often paid in goods rather than money, so that the aid is tied to what the donor country gives.
Advantage – provides major projects, e.g. dams and power stations.
Disadvantage – little value to most ordinary people.

2 Multilateral – money given to international agencies, such as the United Nations, who spend it on health, education and projects.
Advantage – much help given to children.
Disadvantage – large organizations are slow to respond to local needs.

3 Non-governmental organizations (NGOs), mainly charities e.g. Oxfam.
Advantage – more likely to target local needs and run community based projects.
Disadvantage – have to spend too much money on relief aid.

The most useful aid to LEDCs is long-term aid, which funds projects to improve standards of living and increase economic development. The UN's work has done much to improve health care with programmes for immunization, family planning, clean water supplies and sanitation, particularly in rural areas. NGOs have led many village projects to help

This pattern of trade between MEDCs and LEDCs began when many African and South American countries were colonies. Colonies were set up to supply foods and raw materials to the mother countries in Europe.

Even the prices of essential primary products, such as crude oil, go up and down.

Look at Figure 2 on page 108.

In recent years the world price of many commodities has gone down.

Relief aid is short term aid.

After a natural or human disaster, its purpose is to relieve human suffering.

Food, medicines, clothing, blankets and tents are supplied.

farmers increase food output by giving advice, supplying improved seeds and setting up low-technology irrigation systems. Food aid is expensive and people become dependent on it. The way forward is through aid which emphasizes sustainable development for the local communities.

Know your case study

Aid for Ethiopia
Key facts:

1980s
- Relief aid for the effects of drought.
- Over £100 million was donated helped by special fund raising events such as Band Aid and Live Aid.
- Mainly distributed as food aid.

1990s
- Still some relief aid in drought years.
- NGOs, such as CAFOD, have set up programmes for local farmers to increase food output.
- Measures include
  - finding quality seeds suitable for dry years
  - digging ponds and wells
  - loans for buying tools

Test Yourself

1 What are the differences between
   (a) bilateral and multilateral aid?
   (b) short term and long term aid?

2 Make a list of the disadvantages of aid.

Examination practice question

(a) Figure 1 shows development data for three South American countries.

Factor	Argentina	Bolivia	Peru
Birth rate (per 1000 per year)	20	35	26
Natural increase (per year)	1.3%	2.4%	1.8%
Infant mortality rate (per 1000)	23	71	52
Employed in agriculture	12%	47%	36%

◀ Figure 1

(i)   What is meant by infant mortality rate? (1 mark)

(ii) How is natural increase calculated? (2 marks)

(iii) Which one of the three countries is the least economically developed? (1 mark)

(iv) Explain your answer to part (iii) by referring to two of the factors in Figure 1. (4 marks)

(b) Study Figure 2 which shows the prices of crude oil over a ten year period.

(i)   Crude oil is a primary product. Explain what this means. (2 marks)

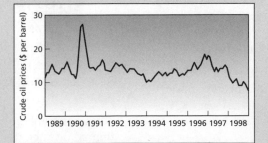

▲ Figure 2

(ii) Describe the pattern shown in Figure 2. (4 marks)

(iii) Some LEDCs rely upon the export of crude oil for more than 90 per cent of their export earnings. Explain the bad effects for them of the changes in oil prices. (3 marks)

(c) Explain how long-term aid may help LEDCs to become more developed. Illustrate your answer by reference to examples. (8 marks)

[Check your answers on page 127]

Total: 25 marks

Summary

Key words from the syllabus

aid	political aid
charitable aid	product dependency
development	short-term aid
GNP (Gross National Product)	tied aid
hazard	trade
interdependence	trade grouping
long-term aid	

Test Yourself

Write down a definition for each of the key words. Check them with those given on page 102.

Check-list for revision

	Understand and know	Need more revision	Do not understand	Hints and tips
know the position of the line dividing North and South	☐	☐	☐	p 210
understand what is meant by economically developed	☐	☐	☐	p 211
know what the letters GNP stand for	☐	☐	☐	p 212
know how to use health, population and literacy as social measures of development	☐	☐	☐	pp 213-15
can give examples of environmental hazards	☐	☐	☐	pp 216-17
understand why clean water is needed to stop disease	☐	☐	☐	pp 218-19
know what is meant by a primary product	☐	☐	☐	p 220
understand the general pattern of world trade	☐	☐	☐	p 222
can explain what is meant by interdependence	☐	☐	☐	p 222
know why world trade favours MEDCs	☐	☐	☐	p 223
know the difference between bilateral and multilateral aid	☐	☐	☐	p 226
understand the differences between short and long-term aid	☐	☐	☐	p 227
can give examples of the aid work of charities (NGOs)	☐	☐	☐	pp 227, 229, 231

Hints and Tips!

The page numbers refer to where the topic can be found in your text book *Understanding GCSE Geography*. If you don't understand the topic read the relevant section in your text book, make some notes and learn about it.

Test Yourself

Tick the boxes and fill in the gaps – if you still do not understand seek help from your teacher.

Know your case studies

Which real places have you studied as an example of...
- a tropical disease   name:_____   pp 218-19
- aid   name:_____   pp 228-9

14 Skills for SEG Syllabus A

OS map skills and other skills are tested in Section A of the first geography written paper. There are also some skills marks in the other questions on both examination papers.

Some of the most important skills are covered in this chapter, especially those connected with maps and photographs.

Ordnance Survey maps

Using a map key

Ordnance survey maps use a series of symbols to indicate features of the landscape. In the examination you will be given a key to the symbols. Make sure you use it to accurately interpret the map. However, you will do even better if you can at least recognize some of the symbols without looking them up. Take care with the following symbols which are often confused:

Roads: motorways are blue; main roads are red; minor roads yellow or orange
Beacons and lighthouses

Aqueducts and bridges
Post Office and parking
Coniferous wood and mixed wood
Windmill and windpump

Grid references

These are used to locate areas and features on maps. Four-figure grid references give the reference for a grid square on a map. Six-figure grid references are more accurate and pin-point a 100 metre square area within a grid square. Figure 1 shows you how to give a four and six-figure grid reference.

> ### Hints and Tips!
>
> North, south, east and west are the four main compass points, north and south being the most important. To work out the compass points in between, the most important points are put first. So, for example, the point between east and south-east is east south east. East is put first.

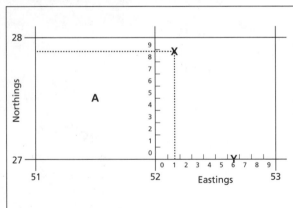

Four-figure grid reference
Give the number of the line forming the left hand side of the square (easting) followed by the number of the line forming the bottom of the square (northing)
Four-figure grid reference for A is 5127

Six-figure grid reference
Give
• the easting (as in four-figure grid reference)
• the number of tenths along
• the northing (as in four-figure grid reference)
• the number of tenths up.
Six-figure grid reference for
X = 521278; Y = 526270

◀ Figure 1 How to give a four and six figure grid reference

Compass direction

As a minimum you should know eight points of the compass although it would be better to know the 16 shown on Figure 2.

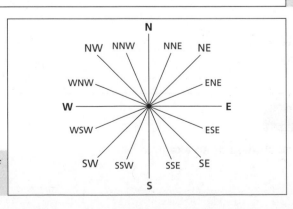

▶ Figure 2 The 16 points of the compass

> ### Hints and Tips!
>
> Which is west and which is east? Remember they spell **WE** across or use one of these acronyms:
>
> **N**aughty **E**lephants **S**quirt **W**ater
>
> **N**ever **E**at **S**hredded **W**heat

Scale and measuring distances

In the examination the Ordnance Survey map may have a scale of 1:50 000 or 1:25 000.

1:50 000 This means that one centimetre on the map = 50 000 centimetres on the ground or 2cm on the map represents 1 kilometre on the ground.

1:25 000 This means one centimetre on the map = 25 000 centimetres on the ground or 4cm on the map represents 1 kilometre on the ground.

The extract in the examination will have a linear scale drawn at the bottom of the map. Figure 1 shows how it would look on a 1:50 000 map.

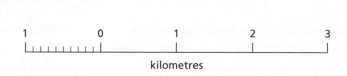

◀ *Figure 3 The linear scale on a 1:50 000 map*

The linear scale is used to accurately measure distances on a map. You may be asked to measure a straight line distance or a winding distance. Use the edge of a piece of paper to accurately measure the distance on the map. Transfer the paper to the linear scale, putting the left hand mark on the 0. Measure the number of full kilometres. Put the right hand mark on the 0 and measure the number of metres. Add the two together for your final answer.

Sketching a cross section

A cross-section shows the shape and height of the landscape. A sketch cross-section does not have to be drawn accurately but its shape should represent the shape of the landscape. Use the contour lines, spot heights and trig. points to help you draw a cross-section. Figure 4 shows a sketch cross-section.

All OS maps have north at the top.

All grid squares on OS maps measure 1 square kilometre – use to estimate distances on a map and as a check that the distance you have measured accurately is sensible.

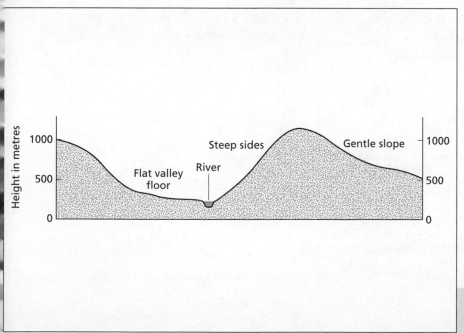

◀ *Figure 4 A sketch cross-section*

Describing physical and human features from maps

There are bound to be questions in the skills section which ask you to describe features on the map. You may be asked to describe:

- Relief – the height and shape of the land
- Drainage – the surface water features, e.g. rivers, lakes, marsh
- Vegetation – includes the obvious green wooded areas but look out for [symbol] which means rough grassland. On the 1:25 000 map vegetation is shown in much more detail – check the symbol key carefully
- Land use – what the land is used for
- Settlement – its location (where it is); its shape (linear, star-shaped, nucleated) and the pattern (nucleated, dispersed, evenly spread)
- Patterns of communication – remember this includes railways and canals as well as roads.

Describing relief

To describe the relief on a map you need to use contour lines, spot heights and trig. points. It is useful if you can recognise simple contour patterns like those shown in Figure 1.

Cover up this page.
What is meant by:

- relief
- drainage
- vegetation
- land use
- settlement
- communication patterns?

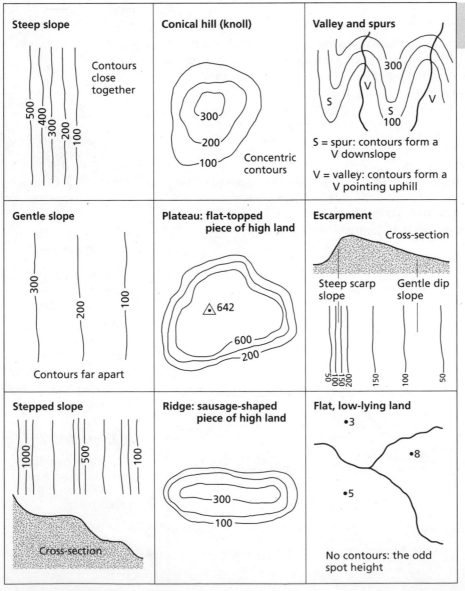

◀ Figure 1 Simple contour patterns

Check-lists for describing features on maps

Relief	Drainage
Contour patterns (Figure 1)	Number of rivers
Landforms	Direction of flow
Steepness of slopes	Width
Heights (general height, maximum, lowest)	Straight or winding
	Tributaries
Valleys – number, shape, valley floor, gradient	Human influence – straightening etc
	lakes and marsh

Vegetation	Communications
Woodland – location, amount, plantations or natural, windbreaks	Types
	Direction
	Landforms followed or avoided
Rough pasture – location, amount	Influence of settlement

Settlement	Land use
Site – height, slope, landform, water supply, resources	Includes settlement, vegetation and communications but also industry, recreational areas and agriculture
Situation – relate site to relief and drainage and other settlements route focus, bridging point	
Shape – linear, star shaped, dispersed, nucleated	

Sketch maps

A sketch map simplifies what is shown on an Ordnance Survey map by only showing the features that are of interest. By the time you take your exam you should be able to produce a neat, labelled sketch map in a matter of minutes. The basic guide-lines are:

- draw a box the same shape as that of the map area you are using;
- sketch in the main relief features, the main rivers, the coastline (if any) and the main lines of communication (use colour to really make an impression);
- mark and label (or add a key) the main features your sketch map needs to show;
- add a title and a north sign.

Figure 2 is an example of a sketch map drawn to show the site and situation of Child Okeford, a small village in Dorset.

Hints and Tips!

The best examination answers always include specific information from the map in the answer, e.g. named places and locations using four and six-figure grid references.

Hints and Tips!

The exam question which asks you to 'Describe the pattern of...' often catches people out.

Pattern means distribution. If you were asked to describe the pattern of settlement you need to say where the settlements are on the map and where they are not. Look for generalizations, e.g. most of the settlements are near the coast, there are no settlements on the upland areas to the west.

Hints and Tips!

Rather than adding one word labels try to annotate your sketch map. This means writing more detailed labels which really do describe what your sketch map is showing.

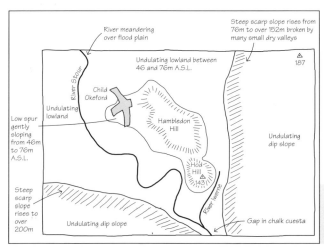

Figure 2 The site and situation of Child Okeford.

Using maps and photographs together

As well as the Ordnance Survey map you may also be given a photograph of part of the area shown on the OS map. The first thing to do is to make sure you orientate the photograph correctly so you know exactly which part of the map is shown. Figures 1 and 3 show an aerial photograph of Berwick-upon-Tweed and a 1:50 000 OS map extract of the east coast of England.

To orientate a map and photograph:

- keep the map facing north

- move the photograph until it is lined up with the same features on the map.

◄ *Figure 1 Aerial photograph of Berwick-upon-Tweed*

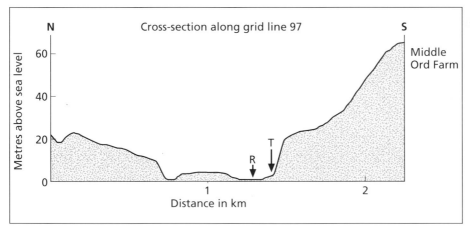

◄ *Figure 2 Cross-section*

Examination practice questions

Study the OS map, Figure 3.

1   (a) In which direction is the River Tweed flowing? (1 mark)
    (b) Give the six-figure grid reference for the railway station in Berwick. (2 marks)
    (c) Describe the tourist attractions in Berwick. (4 marks)
    (d) Measure the distance along the railway line shown on the map. (2 marks)

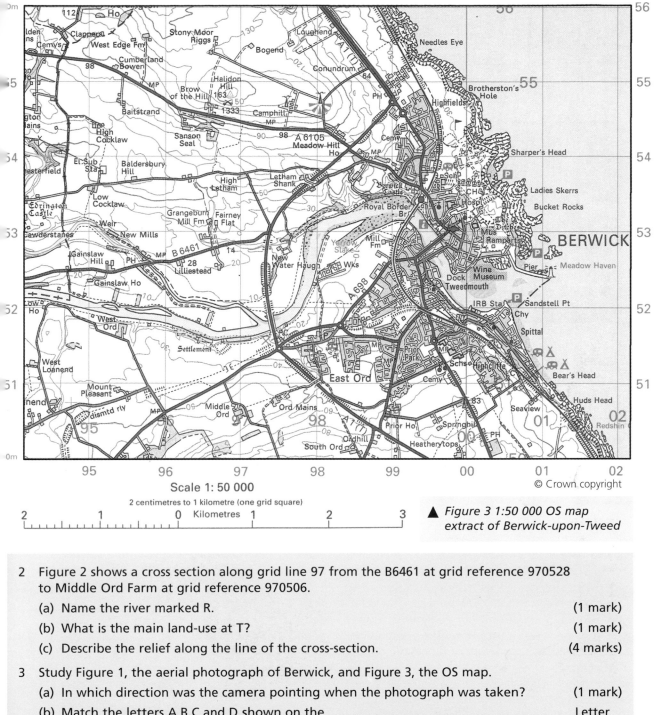

Scale 1: 50 000

2 centimetres to 1 kilometre (one grid square)

2   1   0   Kilometres   1   2   3

© Crown copyright

▲ Figure 3 1:50 000 OS map
extract of Berwick-upon-Tweed

2   Figure 2 shows a cross section along grid line 97 from the B6461 at grid reference 970528
    to Middle Ord Farm at grid reference 970506.

    (a) Name the river marked R.   (1 mark)

    (b) What is the main land-use at T?   (1 mark)

    (c) Describe the relief along the line of the cross-section.   (4 marks)

3   Study Figure 1, the aerial photograph of Berwick, and Figure 3, the OS map.

    (a) In which direction was the camera pointing when the photograph was taken? (1 mark)

    (b) Match the letters A,B,C and D shown on the   Letter
        photograph with the following features: The old city walls   ☐
                                                     The new dock (built 1872-77) ☐
                                                     Railway bridge   ☐
                                                     River Tweed   ☐

                                                                                (4 marks)

    (c) What evidence is there on the map and the photograph that the mouth of the
        River Tweed is tidal?   (2 marks)

    (d) Describe the pattern of roads shown on the map extract.   (3 marks)

                                                              Total = 25 marks

◀ *Figure 1 An aerial photograph of Corfe Castle*

Hints and Tips!

Follow the example of candidate 2 and give more information than you think is needed. That way you make sure of the marks – provided what you write answers the question!

Turn back to the map of Berwick on page 115.

Draw and label a sketch map to explain the location of Berwick-upon-Tweed.

Other skills with photographs
Turning pictures into words

Figure 1 shows an aerial photograph of Corfe Castle in Dorset. The examination question asked the candidates to:

'Describe the layout of the settlement of Corfe Castle   (3 marks)'

What would you have written? Here are the answers two candidates wrote:

Candidate 1: *'It is long, small.'*
Examiner's comments: 'The answer gained 1 mark of the 3 available. The answer is not a description but a list of two words. Long is just about acceptable but small does not really say anything about the layout. A candidate rarely gets more than 1 mark for a list.'

Candidate 2: *'Corfe Castle can be seen in the foreground of the photo on raised· ground.* ✓ *The settlement lies behind the castle* ✓ *and mainly stretches along two roads* ✓ *away from the castle in a linear fashion.* ✓
Examiner's comments: 'The answer gained all 3 marks. It is a proper description and uses proper geographical words such as linear. The description is accurate and makes good use of the photograph. There are four clear points made about the layout – more than was needed for the 3 marks.'

Hints and Tips!

The question asked for explanation so more than one word labels were needed. Detailed labels or annotation was the key to the success.

Sketches from photographs

Sometimes the question will ask you to draw and label a sketch using a photograph. Sometimes the sketch may have been drawn for you and you need to complete it and/or label it.

Figure 2 shows a completed sketch of the photograph of Corfe Castle. The question that was asked was: 'Draw and label a sketch of Figure 1, to explain the site of Corfe Castle.'

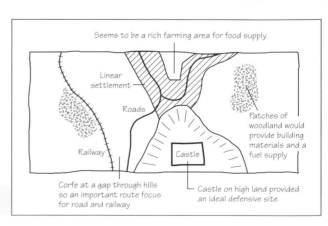

▶ *Figure 2 The site of Corfe Castle*

Different types of maps

Dot maps – show the distribution of actual numbers of items. In geography they are mainly used to show population distribution. On Figure 3 each dot is the same size and represents 1 million people. The map gives a good overall impression of the world population distribution but it is difficult to obtain any accurate figures. Try working out how many people live in Britain!

Test Yourself

What does Figure 4 show? Complete the sentences correctly by filling in the gaps or deleting the wrong words.

The Sudan is shown to have contributed the highest/lowest percentage of refugees in the world with a figure of _____ per cent. Over half/three-quarters of the refugees are internal refugees. Israel also has generated quite a high number, _____ per cent but none/all of the refugees have stayed in/left the country. Most of the world's refugees come from countries in Asia/Africa. This is shown by the large/small area covered by the continent on Figure 4.

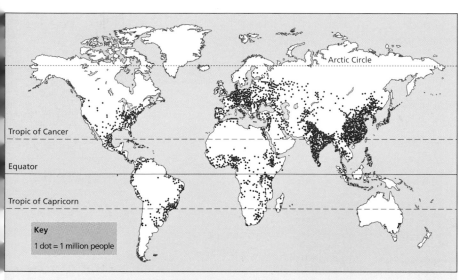

▲ Figure 3: Dot map showing world population distribution

Choropleth maps – these use a shading technique to indicate the density of items in an area. They are often used to show population density. In Figure 4 the choropleth shading shows the proportion of refugees which still live within the country. Darker colours are used for areas with high density, paler colours for areas of low density. The map gives a good overall impression but to gain exact figures for areas are impossible.

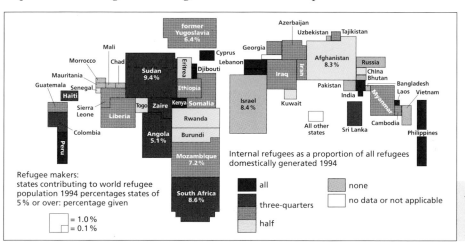

◄ Figure 4 Refugee makers – where refugees come from

Topological maps – these use area or distance to represent other values such as fastest journey times and population. Figure 4 is a topological map. Each country has been drawn according to the percentage contribution to the world's refugee population. The larger the country the more refugees it has generated. The countries have been drawn in approximately the correct positions but their shape is very different from the usual map you would see in an atlas.

Isopleth maps – remember contour lines or isobars or isotherms? These are all types of isopleth maps. The lines join together places with the same height or pressure or temperature. Figure 1 is an isopleth map. It is showing isotherms for July temperatures in Britain.

Can you use and interpret atlas maps?
In an atlas, there are many different maps at different scales. There are world maps as in Figure 2 and maps of countries (Figure 3) or parts of countries. The maps may show a whole variety of information such as population density, land uses or physical features.

◀ *Figure 1 July isotherms in Britain*

Hints and Tips!
Never be put off by seeing a map (or other resource) you haven't seen before. Read the question carefully and apply it to the map.

▼ *Figure 2 World distribution of aid*

Examination questions based upon atlas maps generally fall into two categories:

- Short-answer questions. For example, which country has the highest population density? Give the latitude and longitude of London.
- Longer-written answers which ask you to describe patterns and distributions or even to compare two maps.

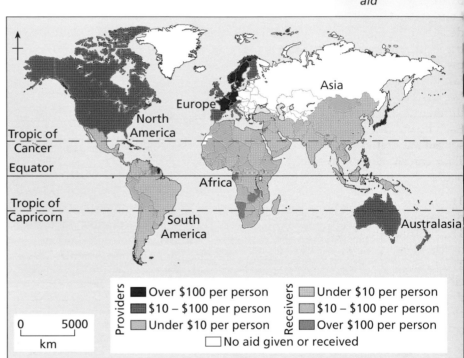

Skills practice question

Use Figure 2 to answer these questions:

1 (a) Which continent is the largest provider of aid (measured in $ per person)   (1 mark)
   (b) How much aid does the UK provide to other countries?   (2 marks)
   (c) Name a line of latitude shown on Figure 2 which passes through South America.   (1 mark)
   (d) Suggest one reason why some countries neither give nor receive any aid.   (1 mark)
   (e) Describe the pattern of aid in the world.   (5 marks)

Use Figure 3 to answer these questions:

2 (a) What is the height of the land in East Anglia?   (2 marks)
   (b) What is the annual rainfall in London?   (2 marks)
   (c) What is the maximum height of the land in Devon and Cornwall?   (2 marks)
   (d) Describe the relationship between rainfall and relief in Britain.   (4 marks)

[Check your answers on page 127]   Total: 20 marks

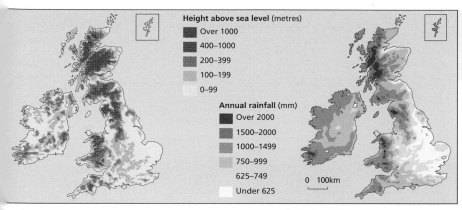

▲ *Figure 3 Maps of the United Kingdom showing rainfall and relief*

Satellite images

Satellite images are taken from space by man-made satellites such as Landsat and Meteosat. Landsat is designed to collect information about the land uses on the Earth's surface. It produces images showing forest, farmland and urban areas (Figure 4). Meteosat is designed to show differences in cloud cover and type. Each image can cover thousands of square kilometres of land and/or sea. They can show patterns which could not be seen by any other method.

The meteosat image in Figure 5 shows differences in cloud cover and type. The centre of the depression is to the north where there is a swirl of cloud. The fronts show up as trailing lines of cloud on the southern side of the depression. The white speckles of cloud are shower clouds behind the cold front.

Hints and Tips!

You don't need to study these if you haven't done the weather and climate section. There will never be a question on weather satellite photographs in Section A on the first written paper. A sigh of relief I hear! – but there may be a Landsat image!

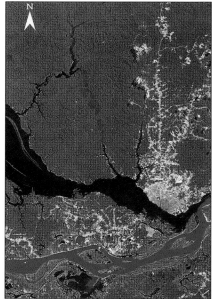

◄ *Figure 4 Satellite image of part of the Amazon Basin near Manaus*

Key:
- settlement – the largest area is Manaus with a population over two million
- the River Negro tributary joining the Amazon east of Manaus
- the vast area of Amazon rainforest
- the river Amazon and its tributaries

Latitude and longitude

Lines of latitude and longitude are just like the grid lines on OS maps (Figure 6). They are imaginary lines which help us to find our way around the world. Lines of latitude run from west to east. The most well known line of latitude is the Equator or 0 degrees. Lines of longitude run from north to south, 0 is the most famous – the Greenwich Meridian which is used by many countries to set time.

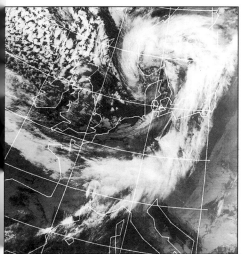

▲ *Figure 5 Satellite image of a frontal depression crossing Europe*

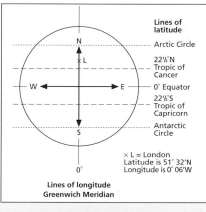

▲ *Figure 6 Latitude and longitude*

Graphs, graphs and more graphs

It is almost impossible to imagine a Geography exam paper without a graph being included somewhere. You should know the different names of the graphs and how to complete each one.

Bar charts (Figure 1)

How to draw one:

- Check the size of the values
- Draw a frame with two axes
- Label each axis
- Plot the scale on the vertical axis (y axis)
- Draw bars of equal width.

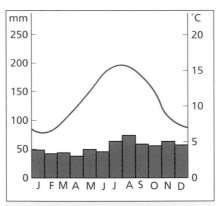

▲ Figure 1 Climate graph for Manchester

Test Yourself

Draw a sketch weather map from the satellite photograph, figure 5 on page 119. Mark on the positions of the warm and cold fronts, the centre of the depression and the area of showers.

(Figure 2B on page 83 in *Understanding GCSE Geography* gives the solution.)

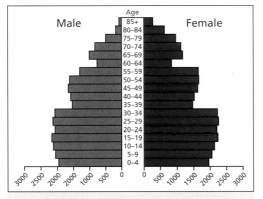

▲ Figure 2 Population pyramid graph

Hints and Tips!

Make sure you have this equipment with you for the examination:

- sharp pencils
- rubber
- ruler
- protractor
- coloured pencils
- pencil sharpener.
- calculator

DID YOU KNOW?

Rainfall bars are always vertical but bars in a population pyramid are always horizontal (Figure 2).

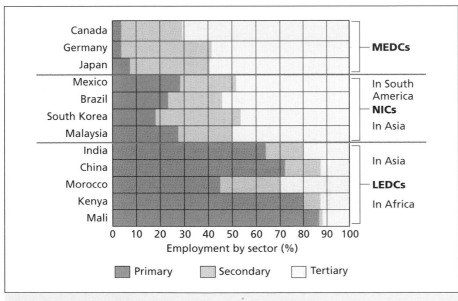

▲ Figure 3 Divided bar chart showing the employment structures for selected countries

Hints and Tips!

On most exam papers the axes will have been drawn for you and all you need to do is complete the bars.

Sometimes, divided bar charts (Figure 3) are used. Each bar is subdivided into parts for example, the land uses on a farm. If you are asked to complete a divided bar chart always copy the shading already used. Otherwise, label your sections clearly or add a separate key.

Line graphs

These are used when the data is for different dates or for different times of the year. The temperature graph on Figure 1 is a line graph showing how the temperature varies from one month to the next. From a line graph you can comment on:
- the amount of change from the size of the differences shown
- the rate (or speed) of change from the relative steepness of the line.

How to complete a line graph:
- plot the values with a clear dot or cross where the two values meet
- join up the dots or crosses with a line.

Pie charts

Pie charts (Figure 4) are used whenever a total can be divided into separate parts, e.g. different types of housing or land use or employment structures.

How do you draw it?
- Values are best in percentages
- Multiply each % by 3.6 (1% = 3.6°, 10% = 36°)
- With a protractor plot the largest segment first starting at 12 o'clock
- Move clockwise plotting from large values to small (always leave 'others' until last regardless of size)
- Colour or shade the segments and add a key or labels

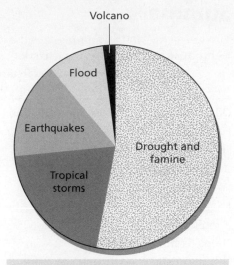

▲ *Figure 4 Pie chart showing the percentage loss of life from natural hazards, 1969-1993*

Scatter graphs

These are used to show a relationship between two sets of data, e.g. temperature and height of the land; GNP and literacy.

How do you draw it?
- Draw and label the graph axes. (The dependent variable should be on the horizontal (Y) axis, the independent variable on the vertical (X) axis.)
- Choose suitable scales for each axis
- Plot the points by dots or crosses
- DO NOT join up the dots

There are three types of relationship or correlation possible (Figure 5).
- A positive correlation as in Figure 5A where as distance to place of work increases so does the journey time.
- A negative correlation as shown in Figure 5B where as the distance from the source increases the size of the pebbles decreases.
- No correlation as shown in Figure 5C where no relationship can be seen.

If a correlation is present it is possible to add a line of best fit to the graph. Draw the line so that an equal number of points lie either side of it. It is even more accurate if you draw the line so it passes through the point where the average value for each set of data crosses.

On a scatter graph, height or altitude is always on the vertical axis although it is often the independent variable.

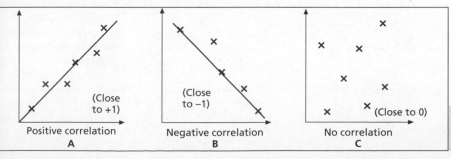

◄ *Figure 5 Types of correlation*

Summary

The following matrix summarizes the skills listed in the SEG A syllabus. The list does not include the techniques and skills connected solely with data collection for fieldwork.

	Understand and can do	Need more practice	Do not understand	Hints and tips
OS Map Skills (1:25 000 and 1:50 000)				
Four-figure grid references	☐	☐	☐	p 110
Six-figure grid references	☐	☐	☐	p 110
Using a map key	☐	☐	☐	p 110
Compass direction	☐	☐	☐	p 110
Straight-line distances	☐	☐	☐	p 111
Winding distances	☐	☐	☐	p 111
Simple contour patterns	☐	☐	☐	p 112
Sketching and constructing a cross section	☐	☐	☐	p 111
Sketch maps	☐	☐	☐	p 113
Describing relief	☐	☐	☐	pp 112-13
Describing drainage patterns	☐	☐	☐	pp 112-13
Describing vegetation	☐	☐	☐	pp 112-13
land use	☐	☐	☐	pp 112-13
patterns of communication	☐	☐	☐	pp 112-13
location, shape and pattern of settlement	☐	☐	☐	pp 112-13
*Recognising and describing:				
fluvial features	☐	☐	☐	See
glacial features	☐	☐	☐	relevant
coastal features	☐	☐	☐	chapter
Other maps				
Latitude and longitude	☐	☐	☐	p 119
Distributions and patterns on atlas maps	☐	☐	☐	pp 118-19
Dot maps	☐	☐	☐	p 117
Choropleth maps	☐	☐	☐	p 117
Topological maps	☐	☐	☐	p 117
Isopleth maps	☐	☐	☐	p 117
*Weather maps and symbols	☐	☐	☐	p 120
Graphs				
Bar charts	☐	☐	☐	p 120
Pie charts	☐	☐	☐	p 121
Divided bar charts	☐	☐	☐	p 120
Line graphs	☐	☐	☐	p 121
Scatter graphs	☐	☐	☐	p 121
Photographs and sketches				
Labelling and annotation	☐	☐	☐	p 114
Interpreting satellite and aerial photographs	☐	☐	☐	pp 119-20
Using maps and photographs together	☐	☐	☐	pp 114-15

Hints and Tips!

The page numbers refer to where the topic can be found in **this revision guide,** *Revise for Geography GCSE.* If you don't understand the topic read the relevant section in the text book, make some notes and learn about it.

Tick the boxes and fill in the gaps – if you still do not understand seek help from your teacher.

* These skills are not needed for Section A on the first exam paper, but if , for example, you have studied rivers you should be able to describe a river and its valley from a map or if you have studied weather and climate you should be able to answer questions on weather maps. You may be asked to do this in Section B of the first exam paper.

Answers to questions

Chapter 1 Tectonic activity
Page 12
Examination practice question
1 (a) (i) Chile   (1 mark)
   (ii) There is no relationship between strength and number of deaths = 1 mark.
         Second mark for giving an example from the table, e.g. the second largest earthquake in the table caused just one death; or an elaboration, e.g. earthquakes of low strength can often kill many people especially if they occur in an urban area.   (2 marks)
   (b) One to two marks for one to two simple points, e.g. more people, less emergency services.
        Up to four marks for clear statements, e.g. in urban areas many buildings may collapse killing more people;
        For five or six marks your statements must be clear and include both LEDCs and urban areas. The very best answers will refer to actual examples.   (6 marks)
   (c) (i) One mark for the fold mountain range and one for the location, e.g. the Alps in Europe/Andes in South America/ Rockies in North America etc.   (2 marks)
   (ii) A model answer for this is on page 9.
         One to two marks for perhaps a few brief statements with no diagrams or some poor diagrams with only a few single word labels.
         Three to four marks for better quality labelled diagrams and explanation which has a more accurate level of detail and the correct sequence.   (4 marks)
                                               Total = 15 marks
How well have you done? You need 8 out of 15 for a grade C and 12 for a grade A.

Chapter 2 Rocks and Landscape
Page 19
Examination practice question
(a) Where? On the sea bed = 1 mark
     How? Sediments are compressed into rock = 1 mark   (2 marks)
(b) (i) The steep slope on chalk needs the scarp label.
         The gentle slope on chalk needs the dip label.
         Vale is the flat area on clay and can be labelled left of the scarp slope or right of the dip slope.
         3 at 1 mark each   (3 marks)
   (ii) Look at the 7 points listed for the formation of chalk escarpments on page 17.
         Each point is worth 1 mark. If you have at least four of them, accurately stated, you will gain the four marks.   (4 marks)
(c) (i) For building and making cement – each worth 1 mark.
         2 at 1 mark.   (2 marks)
   (ii) Most likely disadvantages to mention: noise; dust and dirt; eyesore on the hillside (a big hole is made); waste tips in and near the quarry; lorry traffic through the village.
         If you just list disadvantages, without explaining them, you can gain a maximum of only two marks, no matter how many disadvantages you mention. For all four marks, you need to refer to at least two disadvantages and explain each one. For example, the first point above, noise, can be explained by reference to blasting rock away and heavy machines breaking up the rock and tipping it into lorries.   (4 marks)
                                               Total = 15 marks
How well have you done? You need 8 out of 15 for a grade C and 12 for a grade A.

Chapter 3 River processes and features
Examination practice question
(a) (i) High head or drop of water; plunge pool; may be in a gorge; hard cap rock with softer rock below – any two points. (You could draw and label a sketch rather than write.)   (2 marks)
   (ii) Page 23 has the model answer for this. For five or six marks you would need the following in your answer:
         • accurately labelled diagrams

• written work which explains the formation – it needs to be accurate, in the correct sequence of events and to include process information, e.g. the softer rock is eroded by the hydraulic pressure of the water. This is the great power of the water breaking off small pieces of rock.
You need to do more than just name the processes to get the top mark.   (6 marks)
(b) (i) Dams or levées or tree planting   (1 mark)
   (ii) Dams store water, controlling the amount of water in a river. Levées make the river deeper so it can hold more water. Planting trees increases interception and infiltration, so slowing down the rate at which water reaches the channel. Remember you need two points for the full marks here.   (2 marks)
   (iii) Page 28 provides the answer. For full marks you need to answer all of the question – you need to give a case study, e.g. the Mississippi; one or more causes, e.g. heavy rainfall and snowmelt and one or more effects, e.g. lives lost, property damage etc.   (4 marks)
                                               Total = 15 marks
How well have you done? You need 8 out of 15 for a grade C and 12 out of 15 for a grade A.

Chapter 4 Ice
Page 35
Examination practice question
(a) (i) Pyramidal peak is a three-sided slab of rock leading to a pointed top.
         Arête is a two-sided rock outcrop with a long knife-edged ridge.
         1 only stated or 1 from each without making the difference clear = 1 mark
         1 stated for each one and difference made clear = 2 marks   (2 marks)
   (ii) Tarn lake has a round shape, high up in the mountains in a corrie hollow.
         Ribbon lake is long and thin, on the valley floor at the bottom of a U-shaped valley.
         Same marking as in part (i) for 1 or 2 marks   (2 marks)
(b) You need up to four of the points below:
     • freeze-thaw makes the back wall of the corrie steeper
     • explanation of how freeze-thaw weathering works
     • blocks of rock are pulled away from the back wall by plucking
     • the bottom of the back wall is deepened by rotational slip
     • as the back walls of two corries are cut back, only a narrow ridge is left between them
     • this ridge is kept sharp by freeze-thaw on the mountain peaks
     4 at 1 mark each   (4 marks)
(c) Tourists are attracted to glaciated uplands:
     • for the steep slopes for winter skiing and flatter high level benches for locating the ski resorts and facilities – up to 2 marks;
     • for the lakes – with activities such as sailing, water skiing – up to 2 marks;
     • for the scenery – steep and rocky peaks, waterfalls, deep valleys etc. – up to 2 marks.
     To gain the marks, you need to name the type of tourists who come and what there is in a glaciated upland area for them to do and to see. Naming a real example could also be given a mark.   (3 marks)
(d) (i) Any one from:
         • footpath or ski slope erosion;
         • conflicts between farmers and visitors over problems such as knocking down fences, dogs worrying sheep, walking over crops and dropping litter;
         • conflicts between different groups of visitors such as between those sailing and fishing with those water skiing on the lake.
         There are many choices, but hopefully you chose one that you can write about best in part (ii).
         For naming any one – 1 mark   (1 mark)

(ii) To gain marks, the answer must refer to the same problem or conflict named in part (i).

One or two marks for why it occurs. One or two marks for how it can be reduced.

For example, footpath erosion – erosion occurs because many visitors concentrate in certain places (first mark); popular because of its good views such as Striding Edge (second mark), erosion is reduced by making steps in some of the steeper places (third mark). [In this example there are two marks for why it occurs and one mark for how it can be reduced.]

(3 marks)

Total = 15 marks

How well have you done? You need 8 out of 15 for a grade C and 12 out of 15 for a grade A.

Chapter 5 Coasts
Page 42

Examination practice question

(a) (i) Any two from: high waves; have a strong backwash; breaking frequently

2 at 1 mark each (2 marks)

(ii) Any four of the five points listed for the formation of cliffs on page 38 are needed. If you haven't given four points from the list, but have explained how hydraulic action or corrasion work, you may be able to make up for the one or two marks that have been lost.

4 at 1 mark each (4 marks)

(b) (i) Labels on 1B:

Cliff top has moved further back

More loose rock at bottom of the cliff

Loose rock lying on the surface has changed the shape of the cliff

Wider beach out towards the lighthouse

The new beach is about 300 metres wide

Any three labels of this type. 3 at 1 mark each (3 marks)

(ii) Possible answers:

Loss of life from houses, caravans etc. falling into the sea

Loss of and / or damage to property when the cliff collapses

Sea front shops / promenade (i.e. what has been built at the bottom of the cliff) are damaged or destroyed

Loss of farm land

1 mark for each disadvantage or danger named.

Extra marks for use of more detail or use of an example (e.g. at Barton on Sea or along the coast of Holderness).

Three good points made = 3 marks. (3 marks)

(c) (i) Ways of protecting a coastline: one from sea wall, groynes or breakwaters; piling up boulders; works on the cliff face.

(1 mark)

(ii) Reasons:

Height/size of the cliff

Large amount of loose rock at the bottom

Exposed location suggested by the lighthouse

Either two reasons 2 at 1 mark each or 1 reason well explained for 2 marks. (2 marks)

Total = 15 marks

How well have you done? You need 8 out of 15 for a grade C and 12 out of 15 for a grade A.

Chapter 6 Weather and climate
Page 49

Examination practice question

(a) (i) Two characteristics of a frontal depression:
• area of low pressure
• it has a warm and a cold front

2 at 1 mark each (2 marks)

(ii) The warm air is forced to rise.

Cold air is denser and pushes underneath it.

This happens most at the fronts (where the warm and cold air meet).

As the warm air rises the air cools.

The moisture in it condenses into clouds.

Further rising and cooling leads to rain.

Rain falls ahead of the warm front from nimbo-stratus clouds.

Rain falls along the cold front from cumulo-nimbus clouds.

Any five of these points. 5 at 1 mark each (5 marks)

(b) (i) By adding up the values for those dead and missing in Figure 2. (1 mark)

(ii) Filled up the empty reservoirs in Cuba. (1 mark)

(iii) This year – references to bananas, coffee and sugar cane crops spoilt = 1 mark

Next few years – bananas and coffee are bush/tree crops and any new ones planted will not produce straight away = 1 mark for this idea. (2 marks)

(c) Two ways of answering:
• LEDCs not as well prepared for them, e.g. not as many weather stations to predict weather; weather warnings to people not as easy without radios and TVs; houses not as strongly built, people too poor etc.
• more loss of life after it has happened because it is less easy for LEDCs to provide emergency relief with food, shelter and clean water. May have to rely on relief aid from MEDCs which takes some time to arrive.

Using only one of the two ways can gain all marks provided that sufficient detail is given and especially if an example of areas affected is used. From Figure 2, few deaths in USA as people were warned and evacuated before Hurricane Georges reached it. Another example, drought in Ethiopia and why it led to much loss of life. (4 marks)

Total = 15 marks

How well have you done? You need 8 out of 15 for a grade C and 12 out of 15 for a grade A.

Chapter 7 Ecosystems
Page 56

Examination practice question

(a) Living community of plants and animals (first mark); physical factors such as climate and soil (second mark), with links between them, some of which go two ways (third mark). Marks may be gained from labels on a diagram of an ecosystem as well. (3 marks)

(b) (i) Top layer – crowns/tops of the tallest trees

Next layer down – label such as main canopy, or continuous layer, or crowns of the tops of the tall trees

Next layer down – less continuous canopy of smaller trees

Next layer down – shrubs and young trees

Layer next to the ground – ferns or herb (non-tree) layer

Four layers correctly identified and labelled. (You can check on page 94 in *Understanding GCSE Geography* whether your labelling of the layers is correct.) 4 at 1 mark each (4 marks)

(ii) Explanation is mainly by referring to the Equatorial climate. For example, hot all year so many plants will grow (point worth 1 mark); temperatures are around 27°C all year (point worth 1 mark); wet all year so many plants can grow all the time (another 1 mark point); high rainfall/rainfall over 2000mm (1 mark point as well).

So all four marks can be gained from specific references to the climate.

Also some credit can be given for explanation of the rich nutrient cycle created and how it operates – up to 2 marks.

(4 marks)

(c) Possible ways:
• slash and burn as used by the local (native) peoples
• collecting forest products such as rubber and Brazil nuts
• selective logging
• creating National Parks and Wildlife Sanctuaries.

One way named = 1 mark. Further information about it or an example = second mark.

2 ways at 2 marks each = 4 marks (4 marks)

Total = 15 marks

How well have you done? You need 8 marks out of 15 for a grade C and 12 out of 15 for a grade A.

Chapter 8 Population
Page 66

Examination practice question

(a) (i) Population density is the number of people living in an area or per square kilometre. (1 mark)

(ii) Two points needed from:
• in the north and west
• in the upland areas

Named examples, e.g. Lake District, Pennines, Dartmoor

(2 marks)

(iii) Example – the south-east coast of Brazil

Reasons:
- climate less extreme
- coastal location gives good trading position
- large cities
- fertile soils for agriculture
- long history of settlement
- excellent communication links

A brief explanation of each of these would take the answer up to 4 marks.

To gain the last two marks for the question, a named example and more elaboration are needed, e.g. Rio and São Paulo with industries and commerce attract large numbers of people looking for work; or details of the climate; or the nature of farming.

(6 marks)

(b) (i) Population pyramid/age-sex diagram (1 mark)
(ii) Ethiopia has a wider base, it is not as tall, it is triangular rather than straight. You could write the reverse of these for France and mention that France has some gaps at ages 35-44 and 60-64. (3 marks)
Remember to describe – DON'T just list.
(iii) Ethiopia 's triangular shape suggests the country has a high birth rate and death rate. This would suggest Stage 2/3 in the Demographic Transition Model, i.e. an LEDC.
France's pyramid suggests low birth and death rates, i.e. stage 4 of the Demographic Transition Model – a MEDC. (4 marks)

(c) Methods of solving the problems of high population growth:
Reducing population growth:
- family planning policies and contraceptive advice,
- encouraging women to become better educated and to have careers,
- improving health care so fewer children die,
- encouraging later marriages.

Solving the problems caused by growth:
- environmental schemes, e.g. pollution control, soil conservation,
- reducing socio-economic problems, e.g. unemployment and poverty,
- stopping sprawling cities and providing enough space, food, housing and services for the population.

A brief explanation of some of these with passing reference to an example would take the answer up to 6 marks. To gain the last two marks for the question, examples and more elaboration are needed, e.g. reference to some of the details of China's one child policy or Indonesia's transmigration policy or irrigation in Egypt.

(8 marks)

Total = 25 marks

How well have you done? You need 13 marks for a grade C and 19 marks for a grade A.

Chapter 9 Settlement
Page 76
Examination practice question
1 (a) (i) Inner city or transition or twilight zone (1 mark)
(ii) Terraced houses/back-to back/two up two down/no gardens or garages often just a back yard/long straight rows of houses/built in Victorian times or the Industrial Revolution for the workers etc. Any two points. (2 marks)
(iii) The main problems in the inner cities of developed world cities are:

Environmental	Social	Economic
Decayed terraces	Large numbers of	Poverty
Poorly built tower	pensioners/students	Low incomes
blocks	Ethnic minorities	High unemployment
Air and land	and lone parents	Declining industries
pollution	High levels of	High land values
Derelict buildings	disease	Low rates paid to
Graffiti and	Overcrowding	local council who
vandalism	High crime rates	have little to spend
Traffic congestion	Poor community	on improvements
Lack of open space	spirit	

A brief explanation of some of these would take the answer to 4 marks. To gain the last two marks for the question, some detailed case study information or more elaboration are needed, e.g. in parts of the Gorbals area in Glasgow there are few industries providing work so over 50 per cent of males are unemployed. (6 marks)

Notice the question asks you to explain the problems NOT simply describe them. In the example above the unemployment is explained by the lack of industries. Check that you have explained in your answer and not simply described the problems!
(iv) Zone C is in the suburbs – the houses are larger semi-detached and detached and bungalows often with garages and gardens. The reasons include:
- more space for larger houses with garages and gardens
- land is cheaper so can afford larger properties
- more recently-built so more modern and reflect greater wealth

To gain all 4 marks you must have described the housing and how it is different AND given at least one detailed reason. (4 marks)

(b) (i) Any LEDC city would gain the mark, e.g. São Paulo, Cairo. (1 mark)
... but read the rest of the question and make sure you choose the best example which allows you to write detailed information later.
(ii) Characteristics of shanty towns:
- some are close to the CBD
- largest and most extensive on the outskirts of cities
- on wasteland, swamps or hillsides
- unplanned and illegal
- homemade shacks and shelters
- few basic services, e.g. water, sewage, electricity
- few proper roads or public transport
Any three characteristics described – NOT LISTED – will gain the three marks. (3 marks)
(iii) There are schemes in the shanty towns, e.g. self help schemes and schemes in the countryside to stop the growth of shanty towns, e.g. new towns or transmigration policies – opening up of the Amazon basin. (8 marks)
A brief description of one or more schemes would take the answer to 6 marks.
To gain the last two marks, detailed case study information and more elaboration are needed, e.g. the self help schemes in São Paulo in Brazil have building materials and basic services – water, electricity and drainage – provided by the government and the local people build their own homes.

Total = 25 marks

How well have you done? You need 13 marks for a grade C and 19 marks for a grade A.

Chapter 10 Agriculture
Page 84
Examination practice question
1 (a) (i) Subsistence farming:
farming to feed self and family
no surplus
no profit
Examples – shifting cultivators in the Amazon Basin
Any two points (2 marks)
(ii) Intensive farming:
high inputs
high outputs
often small area of land
Examples – Westland flower growers, rice growing in Asia
Any two points (2 marks)
(iii) Any two of: along coast/near Malindi/in the north east/ close to border between Ethiopia and Somalia (2 marks)
(iv) Export for profit/employs large numbers/feeds people in cities. (3 marks)
(b) (i) Make sure you choose a commercial farm, e.g. hill sheep in the Lake District, flower growing in Westland, the Netherlands (1 mark)
(ii) In this question you must explain the factors and have some physical and some human ones, e.g. for hill sheep farming...
Physical factors:
- Climate – temperature: a minimum temperature of 6°C is needed for crops to grow. The growing season is the number of months the temperature is over 6°C. The growing season is very short in the Lake District and the high rainfall, over 1000mm, makes the ground too wet. The roots of wheat and barley would rot.
- Relief – temperatures decrease by 1°C every 160 metres and the uplands are exposed to wind and rain. Steep

slopes also cause thin soils and limit the use of machinery. Sturdy sheep bred for the uplands are the only possibility.
- Soils – the thin, acid, infertile soils prone to waterlogging are best used for pastoral farming.
Human factors:
- Labour – the population density is low so there is little labour available. Hill sheep farming is well adapted to very little labour.
- Market – the local market is very small. The wool can be transported easily as it is not perishable and most of the animals are sold live for fattening in the lowlands.
- Finance – profits are small on many hill sheep farms so it is an extensive form of farming with low inputs and few changes take place.
- Politics – governments provide subsidies and loans to give the hill farmer a reasonable living.   (8 marks)
Without precise details of the farming type as well as both human and physical factors the answer will not gain more than 6 marks.
(c) (i) the artificial watering of the land   (1 mark)
    (ii) Water lifted out of a river by a shaduf and taken by open canals to small fields surrounded by bunds – 3 points needed (one for name)   ·   (3 marks)
    (iii) Advantages of irrigation:
        increase yields – greater food supply for family or to sell for greater profit
        allows double or treble cropping
        can grow other crops not normally grown which improves the diet
        introduces technology which increases skills of people
        Any 3 points explained.   (3 marks)
                                          Total = 25 marks
How well have you done? You need 13 marks for a grade C and 19 marks for a grade A.

Chapter 11 Industry
Page 92
Examination practice question
(a) (i) primary – any one from farming, fishing, forestry, mining, quarrying
    (ii) secondary – any industry that manufactures (i.e. makes) a product that someone else can buy such as cars, steel, clothes, canned and processed foods etc.
    (iii) tertiary – any industry which gives a service (i.e. without making a product) such as shops, hotels, bus and rail, banks and building societies, health and education etc.
    One example for each is needed. 3 at 1 mark each   (3 marks)
(b) (i) Primary has decreased = 1 mark
         By 36 per cent/under half of what it was = 1 mark
         Secondary has increased = 1 mark
         By 11 per cent/has almost doubled = 1 mark
         Tertiary has increased = 1 mark
         By 25 per cent/has doubled = 1 mark
         (Note that in order to gain the full four marks, values need to be given for at least one of the types of employment.) 4 at 1 mark each   (4 marks)
    (ii) Farming, which is the main primary activity, becomes less important with economic development.
         Instead there is a growth of manufacturing industry in factories and services in offices. These are mainly in the towns where the majority of people live in developed countries.
         Two points made along these lines.   (2 marks)
(c) (i) Newly Industrializing Countries   (1 mark)
    (ii) The main reasons are (see page 91):
         cheap labour
         transport near to the main shipping lanes
         markets in Asia are growing
         government welcome for factories
         Brief explanation for each of these would take the answer up to 4 marks.
         To gain the last two marks for the question, more elaboration is needed, e.g. examples of the low wage rates, or reference to a case study example such as South Korea.   (6 marks)
(d) (i) EU, USA, Japan and Switzerland are all MEDCs = 1 mark
         92 per cent in MEDCs and only 8 per cent in others = 1 mark
         2 at 1 mark each   (2 marks)

(ii) Disadvantages – the main four of these are listed on page 92. You needed to state them and explain how each one is a disadvantage. By doing that you can reach up to 5 marks. To gain all 7 marks, you must have named at least one example of a multi-national company and referred to its product(s) or area(s) where it has factories or offices. (7 marks)
                                          Total = 25 marks
How well have you done? You need 13 marks for a grade C and 19 marks for a grade A.

Chapter 12 Managing Resources and Tourism
Page 97
Activity
You were asked to complete the assessment for fossil fuels, HEP and one other of your choice. Two that you might have chosen (nuclear and solar) have also been completed below.

Factors for assessment	Fossil fuels	HEP	Nuclear	Solar
Renewable	✗	✓	✗	✓
Does not release carbon dioxide	✗	✓	✓	✓
Does not pollute the air	✗	✓	✓	✓
Does not cause local environmental problems	✗	✗	✗	✓
Cheap energy source	✓	✓	✗	✗
Long known technology	✓	✓	✗	✗
Simple technology for use in remote areas in LEDCs	✓	✗	✗	✓
Always available – not reliant on the weather	✓	✗	✓	✗

Page 100
Examination practice question
(a) (i) coal, oil and gas (all three needed for the mark)   (1 mark)
    (ii) any value between 6 and 7 per cent   (1 mark)
(b) (i) They are finite, i.e. they will run out = 1 mark
         It takes millions of years for new resources to form, or some further information about why they are called fossil fuels = 1 mark
         2 at 1 mark each   (2 marks)
    (ii) air pollution = only a 1 mark answer [no marks for 'pollution' by itself]
         For two marks, references are needed to two types of pollution such as global warming and acid rain.   (2 marks)
    (iii) Two main reasons – population growth and economic development.
         All marks can be gained by referring only to one of the reasons if sufficient detail is given, although it is easier to gain the marks if both are mentioned.   (3 marks)
(c) The reasons why fossil fuels are likely to remain more popular than alternative energy sources are given on page 97:
    - familiarity – people have used fossil fuels for many years and vehicles and machines are based upon their use, e.g. cars, lorries, electricity power stations etc.
    - cost – oil and gas are cheap sources of energy whereas alternatives still need costly research and development to make them less expensive.
    - plentiful supply – the fossil fuels are not going to run out by 2010 so that there isn't a strong push into finding alternatives.
    One mark for stating a valid reason; second mark for further elaboration or use of an example. Two different reasons are needed.
    2 + 2 marks = 4 marks   (4 marks)
(d) (i) Name = 1 mark for an area such as a National Park (e.g. the Lake District), or a country (e.g. Kenya).
         Location = 1 mark for describing where it is e.g. North West England for the Lake District, East Africa around the Equator for Kenya.   (2 marks)
    (ii) Environmental = physical attractions such as scenery and climate. Although general or vague information may gain one mark, something specific is needed for two or three marks.
         e.g. for Kenya – mention of wildlife and beaches = the 1 mark

general answer. For 2 or 3 marks, names of types of animals that can be seen on safari or details about coastal resorts such as beaches, coral reefs and climate are needed.   (3 marks)

(iii) The problems that are relevant to this answer are given on page 99 under the headings 'environmental', 'conflicts' and 'economic'.
Attempts to reduce their effects needs reference to management which is referred to on page 100.
Marking of the answer:
- If you only give problems in general terms and do not try to relate the attempts to reduce their effects to the chosen area, your answer cannot gain more than 4 marks.
- If you have only explained problems without reference to attempts to reduce their effects, again your answer cannot go above 4 marks.
- In both of these, you have only dealt with one of the two parts of the question.
- For full marks, you need to explain at least two problems which fit your named tourist area and to give ways to reduce the effects of both of them.   (7 marks)
                                              Total = 25 marks
How well did you do? You need 13 marks for a grade C and 19 marks for a grade A.

Chapter 13 Development and interdependence
Page 108
Examination practice question
(a) (i)   The number of children who die before reaching 1 year old per 1000 births (or similar words with the same meaning).
                                              (1 mark)
(ii) Birth rate and death rate are needed = 1 mark
Death rate is subtracted from birth rate for the natural increase = 1 mark   (2 marks)
(iii) Bolivia   (1 mark)
(iv) Birth rate – high birth rate shows lack of development = 1 mark
As countries become richer more family planning is available, people need fewer children to work on the land or look after parents in old age etc. = second mark for one valid reason.
Natural increase – the gap between the birth and death rates narrows with development = 1 mark
Birth rate reduces to meet the death rate which has already been reduced due to improved medical services = second mark for one valid reason.
Infant mortality rate – becomes lower with economic development = 1 mark
Once richer, better medical services can be afforded, or children have more food which increases their resistance to diseases = second mark for a valid reason.
Employed in agriculture – there are fewer farmers with development = 1 mark
More people live in the cities where the work is in factories (secondary) or offices (tertiary), or fewer people are needed in farming because of mechanisation = examples of gaining a second mark for giving a valid reason.
2 factors chosen at 2 marks each   (4 marks)
(b) (i)   Primary product is something obtained from the land or sea (e.g. a crop or trees or fish) = 1 mark, without being processed (i.e. in the form that it was grown or caught) = second mark.
                                              (2 marks)
(ii) Points that are each worth 1 mark:
- the price goes up and down/it is erratic;
- the highest price was in 1990;
- in 1990 it reached about 35 dollars;
- the lowest price was in 1998;
- in 1998 it was only 10 dollars;
- the price went down from 1989 to 1998;
- it fell by 5 dollars between 1989 and 1998.
Any 4 at 1 mark each   (4 marks)
(iii) You can explain the effects from:
- low and falling oil prices – less income, less money to spend on economic development, less government money for public services such as education and health care, fewer jobs... so both the country and the people are less developed/well off.
- prices going up and down – difficult to make long term plans for development; the plans may be started but then

the money runs out; when there were really high prices the country got used to high levels of spending and it is painful to cut back.
Any three points out of all of these for the marks.   (3 marks)
(c) Long-term aid is development aid – so that standards of living can be improved by economic development. Some aid is for improved health care such as:
- improved (primary) health care with immunization against diseases such as TB and polio;
- setting up clinics and giving health education in rural areas;
- setting up and staffing family planning clinics;
- providing clean water supplies and sanitation.
Some is to help village people to produce more food by:
- educating and giving farmers advice;
- providing farmers with better quality seeds;
- digging ponds and wells for irrigation;
- starting community projects for making and marketing.
Mention of a point in the list above or a similar point that is valid = 1 mark.
Developing the point in more detail = up to 3 marks per point.
Answer without the use of examples = a maximum of 5 marks.
If examples are just mentioned in passing such as 'e.g. Bangladesh' = a maximum of 6 marks.
Some detail about how long-term aid is used in countries such as Bangladesh and Ethiopia is needed for a full 8 mark answer.
                                              (8 marks)
                                              Total = 25 marks
How well did you do? You need 13 marks for a grade C and 19 marks for a grade A.

Chapter 14 Skills
Pages 114-5
Examination practice questions
1 (a) East   (1 mark)
   (b) 994534   (2 marks)
   (c) Wine museum, Berwick Castle, camping/caravan sites, coastal area/piers, golf course, ramparts/walls   (4 marks)
   (d) 5.5-6.0km   (2 marks)
2 (a) River Tweed   (1 mark)
   (b) Woodland   (1 mark)
   (c) In the north, land over 20m ASL; gentle slope down to river valley, below 10m ASL; land then rises gently at first, then more steeply to over 50m ASL   (4 marks)
3 (a) North   (1 mark)
   (b) C = old city walls; B = the new dock; A = railway bridge; D = River Tweed   (4 marks)
   (c) Mud flats; black outline to estuary on map   (2 marks)
   (d) Main A roads lead into the centre of Berwick; outer ring road/bypass surround Berwick; smaller/minor roads dense in areas of housing   (3 marks)
                                              Total = 25 marks

Page 117
Highest; 9.4%; three-quarters; 8.4%; none; stayed; Africa; large
Page 118
Skills practice question
1 (a) Europe   (1 mark)
   (b) Between 10-100 (1 mark) $ per person   (2 marks)
   (c) Equator or Tropic of Capricorn   (1 mark)
   (d) Not rich enough to give but not poor enough to receive. Poor international relations, very low populations.   (1 mark)
   (e) Givers are :
- mostly in the northern hemisphere
- except Australia
- the richer MEDCs
- largest givers are Japan and in Europe
Receivers are:
- mostly in southern hemisphere
- except for north Africa and parts of Asia
- the poor LEDCs
- those receiving most are in Africa and South America   (5 marks)
2 (a) 0-99 m above sea level   (2 marks)
   (b) under 625 millimetres   (2 marks)
   (c) 1000 metres above sea level   (2 marks)
   (d) high land = high rainfall; low land = low rainfall. To gain 4 marks examples of places and figures supporting statements would be needed.   (4 marks)
                                              Total = 20 marks

Index